NICHOLS
foods

LEARNING RESOURCE
CENTRE
PLEASE RETURN WITHIN LOAN PERIOD

21st Century Management:
Keeping Ahead of the
Japanese and Chinese

21st Century Management: Keeping Ahead of the Japanese and Chinese

DAN WATERS

PRENTICE HALL

New York London Toronto Sydney Tokyo Singapore

First published 1991 by
Prentice Hall
Simon & Schuster (Asia) Pte Ltd
Alexandra Distripark
Block 4 #04-31
Pasir Panjang Road
Singapore 0511
Republic of Singapore

Printed in Singapore

1 2 3 4 5   95 94 93 92 91

ISBN 0 – 13 – 932344 – 9

Prentice Hall, Inc., Englewood Cliffs, *New Jersey*
Prentice Hall Australia Pty. Ltd, *Sydney*
Prentice Hall of Canada, Inc., *Toronto*
Prentice Hall Hispanoamericana, S.A., *Mexico*
Prentice Hall of India Private Ltd, *New Delhi*
Prentice Hall International (UK) Ltd, *London*
Editora Prentice-Hall do Brasil, Ltda., *Rio De Jeneiro*

DEDICATION

This book is dedicated to my wife, Vera, who is still very Cantonese although she has been married to a 'Foreign Devil' for over 30 years. As a managing director, she successfully combines eastern and western management styles.

ACKNOWLEDGEMENTS

The author is grateful to his son, Barry, for his comments on an early draft of this book. He is also indebted to Carlye Tsui and Annie Chan, both of The PR Company Hong Kong Limited, to the Consulate of Japan (Hong Kong), to Masao Kawai of Pias Corporation Japan, and to other friends, persons and firms who have knowingly or unknowingly supplied information or helped in various ways. In many cases, these people or organisations are named in the text.

CONTENTS

ix

Part III : Conclusions

TABLES

FOREWORD

The Pacific Basin will be the fastest area of economic growth during the 1990s. The economic strength of Japan and the emerging role of the NIEs are important concepts for Western politicians and businessmen to understand. To a limited extent this subject has been discussed in many forums. In this book, Dr. Dan Waters, who has lived and worked in Hong Kong for many years and has spent much of his time researching and gaining an understanding of this important subject, applies his knowledge of the differences between oriental and western culture to their respective approaches to business in a highly interesting and soul searching way. This book brings out the recent success of the oriental style of management and highlights the factors contributing to its success. With the open door policy adopted by China, the Far East represents vast opportunities for investors and businessmen. This is a period of exciting developments and close links between countries and the interdependence between the East and West are ever increasing. The economic strength of the Pacific Rim will influence development around the world, and so it is important that we understand what is happening and capitalize on it. This book offers valuable and necessary insights for those interested in this field of development.

Dr. the Honorable Allen Lee Peng-fei;
CBE, BS, FHKIE, DEng (Hon), JP;
Senior Member Hong Kong Legislative Council;
Member Executive Council;
President, Meadville Ltd., Hong Kong.

PREFACE

The West, with its industrial revolution starting in Britain in the 18th century, could today usefully borrow some management practices from the Post–Confucian, industrialised societies of the 1990s. That, in essence, is what this book advocates. It would certainly be a more positive approach than complaining about the successes of Japanese, Chinese and Korean entrepreneurs which are mainly due to astuteness and hard work.

Previously, their methods were often considered outdated, inefficient and unproductive by western businessmen and academics who continue to analyse and draw up tables of do's and don'ts and merits and demerits of oriental systems. A few Americans and Europeans even go so far as to say that Asians, by western standards, do almost everything wrong, and that Chinese businesses, whether measured in more abstract terms or as 'X' degrees of effectiveness, are not efficient. In spite of disparagement, results speak for themselves.

During the post World War II decades some western countries have been characterised by low productivity, slow growth and industrial conflict. Japan [which unlike the United States admittedly has had a low defence bill, amounting to about one per cent of its gross national product (GNP)] and the four Asian NIEs, however, have had impressive economic indicators. These four newly industrialised, export-oriented countries, namely Taiwan, Hong Kong, Singapore and South Korea, have growth rates which are double those of the West. But an economy is only as efficient as the firms of which it is composed, and a company is only as effective as the personnel and business methods it employs.

Today, there is growing interest in, and it has become fashionable to talk of, learning from the Japanese — with their distinctive management system — and other East Asians. The aim of this book is to suggest that Westerners would do well to examine more closely their recipe for management and technological success. But although a few consultants advocate 'If you can't beat 'em, join 'em!', can these styles really be exported and introduced successfully into non–eastern businesses? There must be a limit to the extent to which the West can be remodelled on oriental lines.

In some cases, observations and comments cited in this book do not agree. This is not surprising. It is inevitable that situations differ and people, for various reasons, hold dissimilar views. To compare and evaluate both sides of an argument can be useful. Similarly, as in the west, although considerable conformity and distinct patterns exist, management customs can vary from Japanese company to company, and from Chinese firm to firm, more commonly than is usually supposed.

For the reasons outlined above, this publication should fill a need, especially as little has been written about Chinese methods of management. It discusses different management systems and shows how some eastern practices can be adopted and adapted to make the western firm more efficient. It is, however, inevitable that, because the requirements of industries and firms vary, the onus to some extent has to be placed on the reader to make the information in the following pages suit his or her own particular requirements.

MAN MANAGEMENT

... one must learn ... everything about (one's) men – their individual capabilities, honesty, industriousness etc ... (and) how (they) behave under a particular set of circumstances ... but (one) ... must also learn that no enterprise can be successful without the incentive and warmth of a ... magnanimous boss who is capable of capturing his employees' hearts.

The late H.C. Ting
Truth and Facts: Recollections
of a Hong Kong Industrialist
(Hong Kong 1974)

CRISIS

危機

The Chinese and Japanese have no single, simple ideogram for the word *crisis*. Their own equivalent consists of the two characters above, the first meaning danger and the second, chance, which reflect the oriental perception of this idea.

It thus seemed appropriate that these two ideograms, which are said to have intrigued former United States President Nixon, are used as a logo for this book. It is to remind managers that when there is crisis and danger there is also OPPORTUNITY.

PART I

危機

OVERVIEW

Chapter 1
Introduction

'Can anyone expect demanding, independent, individualistically minded Westerners to behave like highly disciplined, group-oriented Japanese?' Let us examine Mr Lei's (the surname, appropriately for an entrepreneur, means 'profit' in Chinese and Japanese) words objectively. Although Caucasians develop team spirit on the playing fields and in wartime the Japanese have perfected the *shudanshugi*, 'all together now', spirit in business more effectively. Emphasis on this, together with dedication and loyalty, has been an important factor in the success of the 'Land of the Rising Yen Incorporated'.

Mr Lei, an octogenarian businessman who is ritually polite like an ancient Confucian sage, like several of his generation, after having made a fortune in Shanghai trading with Europeans and Japanese, left the 'grand old city of the Far East' in 1948 before the People's Republic Government came to power. After arriving in Hong Kong with his family, a few key workers, a suitcase of gold bars and other assets, he cheerfully set about making a second fortune. Lei started business in the British Crown Colony in textiles and then diversified into other areas of manufacturing, importing and exporting, and later real estate.

His *nam pak hong* (literally 'south-north firm' or general trading company), another of his business acquisitions, sells Chinese herbs and medicines, dried seafood, dried fruit and nuts, and other 'necessities' in Chinese life. Although Mr Lei has absorbed some western culture he looks far more relaxed in his native surroundings.

According to him, Asians have a special way of working. They have their secrets. Elderly Chinese businessmen, whose work is their life, usually do not retire but 'wind down' depending upon their state of health. This is done after trying to earn enough money to be philanthropic to ensure they are treated well in the next, 'extremely happy' world and so their future generations will receive blessings. Mr Lei stresses that western and Asian cultures and languages are radically different, and Chinese and Japanese, although not the same, are at one end of the spectrum, compared to Americans or Europeans, who again are not the same, and are at the other end.

He sees Westerners as more nonconformist, casual and confrontational than Asians, with work and business life less interwoven. Westerners also call a spade a spade more than Asians with their indirect talk, euphemisms, avoidance of open debate, and use of middlemen to convey instructions. All these ploys are face saving techniques. The differences can be summed up in Table 1.

In the broad sense 'face' has a universal application, and Collins' Thesaurus gives authority, dignity, honour, image, prestige, reputation, self-respect, standing and status as synonyms. The word is, however, complex and has a special connotation in the East. Lin Yutang maintains in his 'classic', My Country and My People, that, in the Chinese (or Japanese) sense, face,

> "... cannot strictly be translated or defined. It is like honour and is not honour. It cannot be purchased with money, and gives a man or woman material pride."

Face is gained by success and reputation, and is lost by failure which sometimes results in suicide. It has a positive

Table 1: Comparison of peoples — generalisations

	Westerners	East Asians
1.	Individual initiative and creativity	Collective and group strengths, loyalty to family, clan or firm
2.	Confrontational, venturesome	Harmony, self-restraint, humanistic, paternalistic, consider the feelings of others, dislike being in a make or break position because of possible loss of face
3.	Questioning, spontaneity	Accepting, self-suppression
4.	Verbal, outspoken, 'tell it as it is'	Non-verbal, conceal sentiments, 'no' is a harsh word
5.	Everyone makes mistakes	Nothing unexpected must happen, mistakes must be avoided at all costs to prevent loss of face
6.	Self–aggrandisement	Self–effacement, modesty
7.	Casual	Formal, conservative
8.	Private life separate from business life	Private life interwoven with work place
9.	Friendships	Intimacy
10.	Raucous laughter	Respectful giggles

social value which everyone claims to some degree. To maintain face people are required to behave in a certain way, and not to give the necessary face to another, however, humble, is rude. If a request is openly refused both sides lose face. One way out is to forget it!

To Mr Lei the Chinese are quite different to the Japanese, although much of the latter's culture originated from the 'Middle Kingdom' (the direct translation of the two ideograms which denote the name 'China'). The Chinese are more materialistic, individualistic and less disciplined, and they have been likened to a tray of loose, dry sand each grain or person doing their own thing. Loyalty is given to tightly-knit, flexible family firms, with managerial positions held by relatives. Nepotism is the norm. Conversely, with the Japanese, loyalty is more towards the work group and the company which is larger than the average Chinese family enterprise. Although there are slight regional differences — you will seldom see a Singapore businessman wearing a suit and tie — Chinese firms are basically run in the same fashion the world over.

Differences between Chinese and Japanese management methods show in numerous ways, including distinctions in planning, organising, staffing and controlling. Because Chinese society is materialistic, productivity and the maximisation of profits are top priority. The Japanese are prepared to accept low profit margins, and they work to create large turnovers and concentrate on increasing their share of the market even at the expense of short-term losses. Quality products and successful social systems within firms are also important. Of course the Chinese also consider these aspects, but, with the Japanese, they are given greater priority.

Mr Lei says that because of the Japanese concept of teamwork the Chinese often joke and say, 'When doing business with one Japanese you don't need to pay too much attention. And even when negotiating with two Japanese we can still afford to think about mahjong and horse racing at the same time. But when there are three or more, all collaborating, then you have to keep your wits about you.'

Without further study, however, it is evident that culture, language and thought patterns are inextricably linked. Also sets of fairly complex, inflexible, control mechanisms and patterns of behaviour, including traditions, customs, morals and priorities, vary, often considerably, from nation to nation. Consequently because of different upbringing and socio-cultural values, and having to act out of character, western businessmen or *kwai los* (foreign devils), as they are known in Cantonese slang (although today offence is usually not intended), may become alienated when travelling or working in the Orient. In extreme cases they can resist acculturation and undergo severe bouts of cultural shock. Similarly, a European or an American sent on a study tour or an intensive course in Japan may not take kindly to 'immersion' — for example having to eat raw fish and bowing.

The Japanese usually attend courses before their first foreign assignments, to stop them from being 'too Japanese'. They are taught to drink and eat without slurping (which denotes appreciation in the East), how to shake hands, and to look people in the eyes, which, if done too frequently in Japan, may be construed as confrontational.

Chapter 2
Business Culture

Without direction and organisation no group of workers will produce much of value, and every society has created management philosophies and practices, whether at national or corporate level, which vary according to culture. Many Japanese believe — with some justification — that they have the most efficient management style ever devised, and countries like Korea and Taiwan, which were both Japanese colonies up to the end of World War II, are in some ways pale imitations of the 'Land of the Rising Sun'. Korea's management style is somewhere between its Japanese and its Chinese counterparts, and other states, such as Singapore, have also gone to some lengths to tailor Japanese methods to their own needs.

With numerous Nippon firms established in the West it is apparent many management techniques are transferable. This applies not just to Japanese companies operating in America and Europe but also to Japanese methods being used within western firms. Suitably modified and applied Asian management procedures can have a significant impact on prevalent problems, such as low productivity, conflict, poor management-worker relations, distrust, alienation and resistance to change, which have plagued some sectors of western industry. With greater attention being paid to human relations there are signs that some countries are moving in the Japanese direction.

Equipped with more modern machines than the Americans, in the post 'big bang' digital impact era, the Japanese are now able to translate new ideas into practice with skill and high industrial efficiency and at a rapid pace. Not bad for a country which, until not so long ago, was a feudal society. For two centuries it cut itself off from the rest of the world until in 1854 Commodore Matthew Calbraith Perry of the United States Navy negotiated a treaty with the Japanese government that opened the country to foreigners. It sent observers to the West and they adapted what they saw to suit their nation's needs. The Japanese modelled their navy on the British and their army on its German counterpart.

Today, they have been described as the most efficient producers. They are able to achieve the same standards of quality and high productivity overseas using modified methods of business management. But in some work cultures, such as in Europe, old traditions and rigid practices often die hard.

Certainly, incompatibilities between East and West and different circumstances which a manager encounters abroad, make it difficult and often impossible to run a pure, or even sometimes a bastardised Asian management system, in another country. There are those pundits who believe management methods are mutually supportive, like the cords of a net, and that if you try and employ two or three techniques on their own, in isolation, they just will not work.

There is some truth in this. There is no point in attempting the impossible and adopting practices which it is patently obvious will not function properly in the West although it may be necessary to employ a combination of some to prevent inconsistency and conflict.

But even if much is too culture bound to be transferable — and some Japanologists still believe the Japanese have never really learned the art of internationalisation and how to act in relation to the outside world — they have been successful in transporting their business style to other parts of Asia and the West. This has been complemented by their own systems of information technology including the necessary hardware, software and know-how.

Yet some Japanese managers, believing their style is more effective than that of the West, admit it has its strengths and weaknesses. But as they are so accustomed to their own superior management techniques at home it is not unnatural that some dedicated supporters want to employ their methods wherever they go. Consequently, some economists will tell you that Japanese firms are not yet true multinationals in character. Nevertheless, most thinking Japanese realise their unadulterated ways of carrying out a task among foreigners abroad will not necessarily work as they may damage the culture and can be counterproductive.

Having had some experience of training in the People's Republic one sometimes wonders what the pure American methods of management, taught by visiting professors will be like in 20 years' time after the Chinese have adapted them to local conditions.

Economic and managerial practices which are not based on the historical and cultural perspectives of a country cannot be expected to take root and will have implications in relation to the environment. Contradictions are frequently not economic but social. One important lesson that has to be learnt — a skill perfected so well by the Japanese themselves with their revisionist school — is that of the need to :

ADOPT, ADAPT AND IMPROVE.

No truly oriental, stereotype management style, in its

entirety, has been successfully transported to the West, and one sees various hybrid systems between pure Japanese methods and Western. Some individuals advocate that a firm should be more Japanese oriented and others that it should be more western. In the end, in order to minimise problems and conflict between the Japanese and locals, an eclectic management style emerges. The Japanese want their firms to blend with the local landscape. And when synthesising eastern and western cultures, which is never easy, the process will be facilitated if one tries to find common ground.

Chapter 3
Multinationals, *Hongs* and Overseas firms

A group of Americans and Europeans, including visiting businessmen, Old China Hands, and three western-educated Chinese, when talking shop, came to the following conclusions: The time is over when multinationals can ignore local values and traditions. The most exalted of international companies can be made to 'lose face' because it fails to make allowances for local culture. Nevertheless, no multinational can afford to be diverted from a global perspective. These contradictions, most of the group conceded, make the art of management coupled with modern technology more diverse and interesting. It also requires managers to be international in education and experience and have sound local knowledge.

Some British *hongs* (large business houses) like Jardines and Swires, that started trading in the East in the last century and have since diversified into shipping, manufacturing, engineering, service industries and numerous other fields, have absorbed some local culture and ways of doing business. They can be quite paternalistic. A department head is often a European and his deputy a Chinese — or vice versa — and although policy may be laid down by Westerners it is often implemented by locals.

Similarly, one of the aims of the Japanese when setting up a business overseas is to find a good, local, right-hand man. A great deal of the eclectic management style emanates from people like him and they are encouraged to develop their own ideas. Overseas, the Japanese realise

17

that Westerners have a great deal to contribute to their organisation.

As another example, many British *hongs* in Hong Kong pay regard to *feng shui* (Chinese geomancy), and the siting of a building and the positioning of furniture and other objects in it have to be watched to keep them and the staff in balance with nature and the universe. The two bronze lions Stitt and Stephen, outside the Hong Kong and Shanghai Bank headquarters, claimed to be the most cost-effective bank building in the world, had to be positioned carefully, in 1986, with the guidance of a geomancer. Otherwise, the prosperity of the Bank and Hong Kong as a whole could have been affected.

All this may sound like mumbo jumbo to the uninitiated. And it is clearly not for export. But it is important to Asian staff. No self-respecting Chinese is going to disagree with a seating arrangement in an open-plan office which has been prescribed by a geomancer. Although businessmen think in different ways, most will agree that contented personnel are necessary in any part of the world.

Foreign firms in places like Hong Kong need to come to terms with *feng shui* and other — to the Westerner — curious aspects of the business environment. But of course similar situations have to be faced by overseas managers operating in the cross-cultural atmosphere of any cosmopolitan city or by a Caucasian working in a Japanese firm in his own country. Similarly, a small Chinese restaurant doing business in London, or a giant Japanese *zaibatsu* or a Korean *chaebol* (large business houses) with their own strategy and patterns of social relations, with branches around the world, have to learn to adapt to the local scene.

The *zaibatsu*, consisting of a group of 20 or 30 inter-
locking major firms clustered around a powerful bank,
were legally dissolved after World War II. But the idea
survives and one does not find anything like the anti-trust
laws working against big business in Japan as exist in the
United States. Although the Korean *chaebol* is run on
similar professional lines, methods employed are not as
advanced as in Japanese conglomerates.

In spite of what is published about protectionism, a
number of western firms have done well in Japan and
these, indirectly, have helped to bring about a gradual
convergence of management styles. Two examples are
McDonalds and IBM. The former is run by Japanese
entrepreneurs with an all local staff and Japanese methods
of management. But storage, food and service are modelled on, and conform to, United States standards. IBM
too, has an all Japanese staff in Japan, from the president
to the janitor. The only Americans to be seen are the
occasional visitors. Although it is an American company,
it takes pride in being able to turn itself into a French,
German or Japanese organisation. The local manager of
IBM (Japan) or elsewhere is given a great deal of auton-
omy.

Some western firms that have set up branches in Japan
expecting local recruits to welcome the introduction of
so-called superior western management methods have
been disappointed. The average Japanese employee is not
convinced that American methods are better. Besides, he
does not like starting work until he has done his physical
exercises on the shop floor.

Japanese manufacturers followed Japanese traders and
started to move to the West in the early 1970s. They went
to places like Dusseldorf in West Germany, which has a

19

large Japanese community and a Japanese Chamber of Commerce. By January 1989, there were 411 plants in western Europe (over 100 of which were in the United Kingdom). Although some of these are large, the average employs about 350 persons of whom only around eight are Japanese. Average capital totals US$11 million. Although only four per cent of Japanese investment in 1984 was overseas, some economists estimate that this will increase rapidly to 20 per cent. Other forecasters, however, expect a slower build up. This is being hastened by the forming of a single market in the European Community by 1st January 1993, or 'Fortress Europe' or 'Maginot Line policies' as the Japanese prefer to call it. They are eager to get a foot in the door before what they see as the deadline.

Japanese companies are being followed abroad by Korean, Taiwanese and Chinese firms. It is not too difficult to imagine them developing and spreading their tentacles as multinationals in western countries in the next century, much like European companies did over 100 years ago. And, as they progress it is interesting to try and imagine how their management styles will change.

One of the best rags to Rolls-Royce stories is that of Li Ka-shing, Chaozhou Chinese and Hong Kong's richest man and the first Chinese to be Taipan (big boss) of an ex-British *hong* — Hutchisons. This conglomerate's wide-ranging interests include telecommunications, property, finance and investment, and trading. The Taipan's right-hand man is Simon Murray, a Briton, author of a best seller and an ex-French Foreign Legionnaire. In addition to Li's other Hong Kong interests, such as his firm Cheung Kong (meaning 'Long River' and signifying eternity), he now has investments in Britain's Cable and Wireless, and in North America. The latter include

20

Canada's Husky Oil, the Imperial Bank of Commerce and the Toronto Hilton and real estate.

Chapter 4
Management Practices

One of the prime reasons for Japanese business eminence is the assistance given by their Government, including the Ministry of International Trade and Industry (MITI) and the Science and Technology Agency (STA). The Administration, banks and industry (especially the *zaibatsu*) all co-operate to achieve economic success at home and abroad. And, as Japanese and Chinese companies establish branches and factories overseas, many of their management methods, as we have said, are exported.

About one-third of male employees in Japan — those in large well-established companies — join a firm after leaving school or university and stay with it, barring unforeseen circumstances, for the rest of their working lives. There seems little likelihood that this practice will die out in the foreseeable future, and one can argue that staff are loyal to their company because no other firm will hire them if they resign. Nonetheless, this is not so true today, and it is now easier for managers in mid-career to switch jobs and to abandon the time-honoured life-time employment system if they see better prospects elsewhere.

But even in the West, in the public sector, the Church, the armed forces and organisations such as some banks, insurance companies and the like, the so-called lifetime employment (sometimes dubbed lifetime imprisonment) method is common. Firms like Unilever and ICI, too, encourage staff to make a lifetime commitment and during the great depression of the 1930s IBM did not lay off any of its staff. But the custom is not followed in

America or Europe to the extent it is in Japan. In fact, many techniques which we think of as being typically Japanese are also employed in the West. Often it is a case of degree.

Japanese businessmen in the western hemisphere insist that they are thinking long term and have no thought of pulling out. They say that they want their companies to be an integral part of the local community, and that they hope to employ the children and grandchildren of the permanent workers who they engage at present. This is certainly something to aim for. Then the families are committed to the company. The Japanese also plan that more western managers will take up senior positions as Japanese executives are transferred home in the future. Nevertheless, key foreign positions are likely to continue to be filled by expatriate Japanese who are segregated from local managers by different scales of pay and systems of employment and promotion.

Again the 'seniority system' is by no means entirely Japanese. It is frequently taken into account for promotion and pay increases in the public sector and in other organisations in the West. It is less common in Asia than it was 30 years ago as employees today expect to be rewarded according to ability. Nonetheless it has been reported overseas that, to encourage loyalty, some Japanese firms have laid down wage structures which favour seniority, and employees with longer service are paid a little more. Yet the Japanese are fond of emphasising that senior positions are, by effort, open to all and a foreman who was once, say, a line operator has the opportunity — like Napoleon's proverbial private soldier with a field marshal's baton in his cartridge-pouch — to become the future managing director. This is not unlike the American dream, 'From log cabin to White House'.

Nevertheless although it is common sense, whether it is the seniority system, lifetime employment, or *feng shui*, we must always remember :

BECAUSE A CERTAIN PRACTICE WORKS WELL IN ONE COUNTRY IT DOES NOT NECESSARILY MEAN IT WILL ACHIEVE THE SAME RESULTS IF TRANSPLANTED ELSEWHERE.

Chapter 5
Small Firms and Convergence

Customarily Chinese businesses are small, and, as an example, in Hong Kong 92 per cent of all firms employ fewer than 50 people. It is also not unusual for a Chinese entrepreneur to 'grow' one Chinese company alongside another. This keeps them smaller, more manageable and flexible, with a strong capacity for survival. Risks are hedged to protect family assets. There are similarities here with Indian shops in Britain, and the Italians with their small management enterprises (SME).

The way the average Chinese firm is run means there is an effective limit to its size: a point of equilibrium beyond which it is not possible to run it effectively. When it is young, small, dynamic and growing, often employing cheap family labour, and left loose and free to cope with changing economic conditions, the pragmatic owner-manager of his one-man band can keep an eye on everything. It is unnecessary to subdivide or delegate. There is scope for creativity and experimentation in an enterprise culture. In times of recession, turbulence and uncertainty, such firms are able to adjust easily, and, while they may wane quickly, afterwards, they often bounce back fast. It is adversity — such as a recession — which illustrates the resilience of a company.

Because business breeds business, these small firms provide any economy with a considerable degree of vitality and dynamism. Prime Minister Margaret Thatcher has advocated the need for 'self-starters' to revitalise the economy by opening new businesses in the United

Kingdom. She believes these hold the key to the industrial future. Holding similar views to those of E.F. Schumacher, well known for his work on Intermediate Technology in Third World countries and who believes that 'small is beautiful', Margaret Thatcher admits that for the man or woman branching out in a spirit of adventure, as his or her own master, business is a life full of worries, but he or she is creating something fresh. This is also the Chinese spirit, and for many the aim is to start their own business. Prince Charles has spoken on similar lines to Mrs Thatcher. Giantism is not always the answer.

As soon as an enterprise reaches a certain size — and this point depends on the type of business — or it diversifies, it risks over-reaching itself and it is no longer practicable to run it on similar lines in its next life cycle. It is also not easy to retain many of the organisational characteristics which enabled the small company to be successful. Chinese mini-firms are usually averse to bureaucracy and their managers try to avoid paperwork.

Although some Chinese organisations are technically public companies they are usually not professionally managed in the western sense. They are more centralized under dominant family influence, and are less standardized, less specialized and less formalized, with minimal objective control, than their western counterparts.

Dick Lei is the 45-year old son of Mr Lei and he will continue the dynasty, but, unlike Napoleon's private, he does not need a 'field marshal's baton' in his briefcase. He has an MBA degree from the United States, and, after graduating, he worked there for eight years. On arriving back in Hong Kong 12 years ago, he set up a factory within his father's empire.

With people like Dick Lei coming back to Hong Kong

a new style of management, which is more 'systems oriented' and more like the advanced industrial nations, has developed. On his return, with a spirit of convergence, Dick was allowed by his father to introduce a number of western ideas. But not to the extent he would have liked. Sometimes overseas education and a judicious blend of East and West do not help bridge the Chinese generation gap. Many young people want to sever links with the past. They don't resent traditions but they believe in evaluating. They prefer to select and combine old and new approaches based on pragmatism and efficiency.

Lei's factory manufactures machine tools, and Asians have to live and compete in a shrinking world, with advanced communications and easier travel, which is dominated by western technology. This technology, often employing complicated equipment, has to be culture free to a high degree and linked with a common methodology of operation and style of management no matter whether it is in use in the West or the East. For instance, although age old Chinese-style hand tools for bricklayers and carpenters may differ from Guangzhou to Glasgow, and a Japanese handsaw (*nokogiri*) cuts on the pull stroke unlike in Europe and America where a saw cuts on the push stroke, machine tools such as lathes, millers and spark-erosion machines are similar around the globe. When these are operated, standard methods, workstudy and rules of safety have to be followed. Although Dick received much of his education in California, which the Chinese nickname Old Golden Mountain, and he is westernised to a large extent, inwardly, he is still very Chinese.

When he returned from overseas, although his father gave him some discretion in setting up his factory and running it, they both agreed to employ a paternalistic

Chinese personnel management style. They do not always see eye to eye, however, and while he and his brother voice their opinions freely, their father has the final say on important matters and the right to make binding decisions. They respect his views. It is normal for the omnipotent father, as corporate leader at the apex of the pyramid, to have the last word.

Most heads of Chinese families believe there is nobody else who can do it quite as well as they can. This sensing of decisions and impulse instinct among Chinese has also been called capitalisation of intuition or informed gambling. With acumen and experience, coupled with perception for timing and 'gut feeling', most Chinese businessmen are ready to take a calculated risk. It is an art rather than a science that cannot be learned in management classes but instead is developed in the school of hard knocks. As Dick so ably put it, like the logo for this book, 'When there is danger and crisis, and opportunity knocks, you need to be able to seize it quickly.'

In humorous vein he quoted the Japanese businessman who for a long time had waited patiently for the moment to introduce himself to a potential client. On hurrying into the swimming pool, in an international hotel, he had the misfortune to bump into a Westerner. But taking advantage of the occasion, after bowing, he extracted his status symbol, a plastic-coated, waterproof business card, from the pocket of his swimming trunks. This was presented, in the correct fashion, to the honourable gentleman. The American knew the drill and studied the card, which reflected the lifestyle of the donor and provided an entrée, before putting it away carefully in his pocket. In the Japanese case the name of the company is usually more prominent, whereas, for the Westerner, the person's name is set in bolder type. It has been estimated that 13 million cards are exchanged in Japan (with its population of 123 million people) every day.

PART II

危機

MANAGEMENT STYLE AND FUNCTION

Chapter 6
Decision Thinking and
Bottom-Up Management

Asians tend to think in complex, contextual, all-embracing ways, first considering the overall, perhaps wide ranging, field of interest. This is then narrowed, although options are if possible left open, until segments are analysed and items pinpointed. When a Japanese or a Chinese writes an address the country comes first, working down to the flat number and the addressee last. Similarly, with dates, the year is written first and the day last. The Westerner would write, in English, in the reverse order. In places like Hong Kong, Chinese books generally still start at, what is to the Westerner, the back, print or writing runs from top to bottom, and lines progress from right to left across the page. With Chinese landscape painting more attention is paid to the picture as a whole rather than to detail, such as tiny figures: traditional Chinese medicine also takes a holistic approach. This contrasts with its western counterpart which is more analytical and concentrates on a specific part of the anatomy.

Again there is a difference in the concept of time. The western executive tends to view it stretching out in a straight path ahead, while the non-westernised Asian sees it as a spiral. This may have something to do with a belief in reincarnation, and the acceptance that there is a time to live, and a time to die, and a time to be born again. It also has implications at work.

It means that when an opportunity or deadline is

missed the Westerner will see it receding steadily behind him into the past. But as time goes by the non-western-ised Asian will, inwardly, expect that on occasions in the future on the helical of time there will be similar opportunities and deadlines within easy reach once again. With such a philosophy stress is reduced.

The outcome of all this, it has been suggested, is that the Asian approach to management and achieving targets is not the same as with Westerners. The cortex of the brain is composed of two hemispheres. It has been propounded by some psychologists that most people's left hemisphere (left-handers excluded) handles thought patterns which need to be processed in a linear, sequential, systematic manner, step by step. The right lobe, conversely, operates in a more general way with simultaneous thought processing.

Some of us are logical thinkers (sometimes dubbed convergers), while others are instinctive thinkers (divergers) giving the impression of being oblivious to careful reasoning. Westerners, it has been suggested, are largely left-lobe thinkers, which makes for a more systematic and rational approach. Contrastingly, Asians are mainly right hemisphere thinkers. They tend to see things in wholes rather than made up of parts and to synthesise rather than to analyse. They subscribe to the view you cannot possibly comprehend totality by looking at detail.

Non-psychologists might be tempted to put the cat among the cockatoos by asking what happens to a Chinese when he is trained or brought up in the West, or to the Eurasian? To what extent does tradition play a part? More research is needed on this interesting topic and how it affects management and decision making.

·The Japanese *ringi* (*rin* means submitting a proposal

and requesting a decision, and *gi* denotes deliberations and actual decisions) system consists of shared decision thinking, where a consensus is reached by the staff involved who can contribute effectively. The Japanese think an issue over thoroughly, define the question (does a problem really exist?), put it all down on paper and pay immense attention to all aspects of *nemawashi* (literally digging around the roots before transplanting). And because the views of many are sought, with consensus management and group consciousness, the decision is likely to be sounder and later implementation made easier because much spadework has been done. It has already been presold and employees are committed. Thus, when the proposal reaches the president he can, in theory, pass it back and say: 'This is your idea, get on and implement it.' With this collective method miscalculations are rare and it suits the Japanese sense of values. It also helps to boost morale, generate harmony and strengthen loyalty and cohesion among staff. Group decisions tend to be bolder than those made by individuals and better represent a long-term view.

But the *ringi* system can be a slow, cumbersome process, and, in extreme cases, is like a giant centipede advancing. It is often vague and indecisive. Because of possible 'politicking' the *ringi* system and 'bottom-up' management can give aggressive western top managers the jitters. A long-time Japanese business associate is fond of telling how his firm lost the opportunity to purchase accommodation because they delayed too long on the *ringi* procedure.

The main differences in the decision-making process of Westerners, Japanese and the more adventurous Offshore-Chinese is outlined in Table 2.

37

What can Westerners learn from the East? Certainly the *ringi* system can be worthy of imitation, in a modified form, in a large company in the West, but the method has its limitations. The information and views generated by the Japanese system are valuable when key strategic decisions have to be made but the mass of detail can hide real

Table 2: Comparisons of Western, Japanese and Offshore Chinese methods of decision making and management — generalisations

	Western	*Japanese*	*Offshore Chinese*
1.	Firms employ 'systems' style management and Management by Objective (MBO)	Firms highly institutionalised, restrictive, protectionist, stratification is a unifying influence	Firms small, dynamic, free-ranging, open, resilient, flexible and adaptable
2.	Individual decision making	Dependence, compromise, consensus, decentralised decision making by group with a ceremonial boss	Decision making by key figure or a few family members — these are often snap decisions
3.	Aggression, conflict, confrontation	Collective responsibility, harmony, competent industrial bureaucrats rather than leaders, manager is facilitator	Intuitive, centralized, authoritative, adventurous management style, autocratic but frequently employing benevolent paternalism

corporate needs and bureaucracy slows proceedings. Conversely the 'top-down' Chinese method, albeit with modifications, usually works well in small firms in the West, when capable managers who have a good grasp of the situation are in complete charge.

Of the Chinese, Japanese and western methods each has its strengths and weaknesses. Much depends on what is required, in what sort of enterprise the system operates, and the availability of resources. Suitable combinations of the three systems may prove the optimum solution, so decisions can be made effectively and speedily at levels where they will have the most fitting impact.

In spite of drawbacks and difficulties in transplanting the corpus of Japanese management methods to America and Europe a few western companies, in order to democratize management, have incorporated unadulterated collective decision making and bottom-up management. Such systems have also been used in the West in government departments and elsewhere, in a modified form, for a long time.

The Japanese themselves have tended to drop such practices overseas and crucial decisions are taken by Japanese executives. They will usually do what they can to avoid decentralising the process and important decisions are normally made in Japan. This means overseas Japanese are often busy telephoning back to the motherland at night. They then come to the factory the following morning saying what has been decided and sometimes trying to make it appear local managers, with their suggestions, played an important part in the deliberations. This again illustrates that Japanese management styles vary.

To be fair, even if Americans or Europeans speak Japanese and understand all the details and implications of the different philosophies existing between races it is not always easy to arrive at similar conclusions. For these reasons, local managers in Japanese firms sometimes feel alienated by what they consider as the high-handed manner in which the Japanese decide issues.

It is something of a paradox, bearing in mind what is written elsewhere in this book. But because of the above factors, and because, overseas, many Japanese bosses remain tightly in control and do not discuss things openly with local managers, some Japanese are seen by Western-ers as autocratic and arrogant. The more vociferous American or European will also occasionally argue that what seems like Japanese 'democracy' is, in reality, a form of autocracy and sometimes — with such incidents as the 'Recruit scandal', in the late 1980s, where high-ranking politicians in the Japanese Diet were bribed by business-men — a corrupt one at that. Nevertheless, the more successful Japanese overseas do delegate and give a great deal of authority to occidental managers.

Chapter 7
Managers

Generally speaking the Japanese manager is not so aggressive or venturesome as his Chinese or western counterparts. He is not expected to be domineering or forceful, and often avoids responsibility and is not likely to upset the lichee cart. He is supposed to inspire and induce confidence.

Japanese leadership bonds are built on mutual obligations between superiors and subordinates. The leader has the task of carrying people with him and supporting and developing good relationships, and a department head represents his colleagues when dealing with other groups. The leader also has to manage the consensus process whereby his department makes certain decisions. His duties should appear as the exertion of a minimum amount of management control, and the fostering and maintenance of harmonious group relations and face to face contacts, coupled with individualistic leadership qualities. The executive is not expected to ride roughshod over subordinates' opinions, and staff can react intensely if, on rare occasions, he dares to try to do so. In exchange for what members of a Japanese unit, which laughs and weeps as one, see as good leadership they will offer loyalty, co-operation and deference.

Japanese managers assume quite different roles to their Chinese opposite numbers. The latter usually employ top-down management style and lead from the front. This contrasts with Japanese enterprises where bottom-up style is the norm and the bulk of the work is undertaken by middle management. In Japan the idea that authority rests at the top, as in the West, is a delusion. However virtue, insight and vision (with broad horizons) rationality, reliability, the ability to co-operate and inspire others and dedication, have been quoted as desirable qualities in Japanese managers. Such attributes are, of course, also sought in the West.

When promotion depends upon seniority, some Japanese believe it is better if the one selected is not too intelligent, extrovert or aggressive. If the leader is too capable and forceful he can encroach upon the role of the group on which, in Japan, so much depends. He is then likely to be alienated from his subordinates. In the West, a manager is judged more on the characteristics he himself displays rather than the overall efficiency of his department, as in Japan. This can be confusing and when attending meetings and doing business there, Westerners find it frustrating not knowing who to contact. With emphasis on group attainment in Japan sometimes it seems no one is really in charge of anything, not even the president.

Chapter 8
Position Power

Position power of managers is characterised by power-distance. This can be classified by the extent to which members of organisations, such as business houses, possess unequal distribution of power. In large power-distance societies employees accept a hierarchy in which the status and authority of managers and those, say, of blue-collar workers vary considerably. In small power-distance societies the work force has usually striven for greater equalisation and is not prepared to accept great power inequalities.

Compared to western countries, Confucian Singapore, Taiwan and Hong Kong are all grouped in the large power-distance category, which means a more autocratic and authoritative style of leadership. Japan, with a larger population has less distance than these three societies because of culture, their democratic political system and greater income equality. Although a Chinese is a Chinese no matter on which side of the Hong Kong/China border he lives, in the People's Republic, because of egalitarian communist doctrine, power-distance between management and workers tends to be low. Naturally some organisations in any country, by design, because of the personality of the manager, or similar reasons, have shorter power-distances than others.

But the Japanese never seem to lose their sense of rank. It is important to them. The ranks do not confront one another; e.g. middle management versus supervisors. There is also less distance between the different grades of their rigid hierarchy. This state of affairs does not exist in the same way with the Offshore Chinese, who accept position power providing they are 'given face', and managers and workers are comfortable sitting down chatting and having a meal together. The real issue, which has consequences for the way organisations are established and run, is how a society manages inequalities among its work force. The Eastern approach has been to combine and integrate successfully the seemingly paradoxical elements of trust, participation and authoritarianism, especially in the case of the Japanese.

Chapter 9
The Atypical Manager

In practice it would seem, then, there is no such person as a typical manager. There is instead a variety, including the strict autocrat, and the benevolent autocrat who tempers his considerable authority with consideration for his staff. There is also the incompetent autocrat who insists on retaining power when the firm could be run more effectively by delegating. At the other end of the manager spectrum we have the genuine democrat, and the pseudo-democrat who sets up committees but still decides issues himself or telephones back to head office. There is also the *laissez-faire* manager who does not provide sufficient leadership and no one is really in overall charge.

Managers may also be classified in one of the following three basic groups. Firstly there is the traditionalist, like a Chinese merchant of the old school who adheres to his Confucian upbringing, and, even after contact with Westerners, does not change his time-honoured practices. Then, secondly, there is the ideologue like Mr Lei who supports Chinese ideology but nevertheless admits the need for vision, pragmatism, and making changes to suit the modern business world. Lastly there is the apologist who, like Dick Lei, while not himself becoming entirely westernised, feels Chinese business methods are inadequate to meet modern challenges and it is necessary to westernise management techniques. In the four Asian NIEs managers in all these categories are common.

Chapter 10
Egalitarianism

Although a few forward-looking western companies have had so called 'classless structures' for a long time they are not common. Most managers, and even some white-collar workers, do not like them. They prefer, if they arrive late, to be able to drive straight into their reserved carparks and to eat in a separate, more luxurious, cafeteria.

Japanese and Chinese firms are not, of course, really egalitarian. There is a rigid hierarchy. Personnel enter depending upon their educational backgrounds, and, for promotion, seniority is important. But in Japanese firms there is only one hierarchy. Also, as Akio Morita of Sony says in his book, 'Made in Japan':

"Today, the salary for a top management official is rarely more than seven or eight times that of an entry-level junior executive trainee."

Because it is a more classless structure, with less discrimination, blue-collar workers in the West accept Japanese methods readily. Although they know the general manager is paid more than them they prefer the Japanese concept where everyone wears the same company uniform. At the start of the day they drive into shared, non-reserved, car parks, and everyone, whether manager, head clerk, mechanic or floor sweeper, takes part in ten minutes of bending and stretching together as soft music is played over the tannoy system. This is not just a case of exercise for exercise's sake, but for inculcating team spirit and getting the group pulling together. Because of some resistance, or fear of being ridiculed, not all Japanese firms insist on morning callisthenics in their western plants.

Nevertheless, in order to promote a one-class workforce, most employees are in favour of shared eating facilities, and shared washrooms and locker rooms, all of which encourage easier informal communications. Company amenities can be extended still further to sports grounds and recreation centres, although many western workers insist they are not really interested in these and what they want is higher wages.

A good example of sense of sharing may be seen at Sony where, with an 'open plan', not even the head of a factory has a separate office, and he, like everyone else, wears the same stylish company jacket. Some resistance was raised in the first instance in England when service engineers wanted to wear their traditional, long white dust-coats. But later, the Sony jacket was accepted and any idea of a separate hierarchy broke down.

One objection that has been raised is that everyone looks alike and a visitor cannot distinguish the manager. In some firms there is no receptionist and all that exists are clear instructions to visitors on how to dial, on an internal telephone, the person he or she wishes to meet.

Another company in Britain that has adopted the single-status system is Toshiba. Here the 'common touch' extends to hours of work, canteens, uniforms and sick pay.

Chapter 11
Team Spirit and Royalty

With the western philosophy of self-interest in mind, the story is sometimes told of the German who worked in a Japanese factory in Europe. After being sent to Japan for training he refused to share the knowledge he had gained with his workmates. His Japanese colleagues who had 'emotionally' merged with, and were prepared to 'sacrifice' for, those of the same culture with whom they worked, could not comprehend it. They did not appreciate that the Japanese maxim; 'As we as a team think, I perform', in the West becomes; 'As I as an individual think, I act.' In America there is the glamorous image of the lone cowboy who believes, 'If you don't go alone you don't get along.' Accent tends to be on performing well, independently, as individuals.

Certainly emphasis is placed from childhood in Japan on being a member of a team. In the summer of 1945, everyone, including women and children, were prepared to defend Japan to the death with home-made bamboo swords. When the war-time Cabinet had authority it was obeyed, absolutely. After the Emperor surrendered and spoke to the nation, General Douglas MacArthur took over, and he too was obeyed, again absolutely. Like priests and Queen Elizabeth's Royal Household Footguards, the Japanese live in a world that honours authority.

Japanese society consists of countless circles, and every person is on the outside (*soto*) or the inside (*uchi*, the character also means home) of various well-defined groups. Besides the family, the average Japanese belongs

49

to a group at his workplace. There is also, perhaps, the karate or flower-arrangement class. The largest circle, it can be argued, ends at the nation's geographical frontiers. Perhaps that partly explains why many Japanese, it appears, are not always at ease overseas in the company of foreigners.

The tradition of collectivism and conformity is obviously not nearly so strong among Anglo-Saxons, where eccentricity is by no means uncommon, and is, up to a point, accepted: unlike in Japan where, at home, in the school, or at work, 'The protruding nail is hammered down.' But when the Westerner 'goofs', and does things wrong, the Japanese generally give him a chance to rectify his action. This opportunity would not be accorded to persons of their own nationality. The Japanese fear the consequences of not conforming. To be insensitive to others' feelings is to be a social outcast.

Naturally these characteristics are carried over into business culture, and, in the average Japanese firm, emphasis is given to building a spirit of mutual trust, shared responsibility, participation in decision making, quality control circles and bottom-up management. With this 'gestalt pattern' the power of the team as a whole, with all persons pulling together, can be far greater than the sum of the constituent strengths of the individual members. Using this method they dovetail together into assault teams which develop a spirit similar to the *Bushido* warrior code. The latter looks upon retreat or surrender as shameful. These industrial assault teams are employed to hurl themselves into the product-development battle.

So, a summary of what we have said so far about the characteristics of the Offshore Chinese and the Japanese — the former with their patriarchal management system and the latter depending more upon teamwork — may be outlined as shown in Table 3.

Table 3: Comparisons of Offshore Chinese and Japanese leadership methods — generalisations

Offshore Chinese	Japanese
1. Firms depend on individuals or small groups of family members or close friends	Firms depend on teamwork, prefer group achievement to personal glory, and collective responsibility
2. 'Who is in charge?' — a response	'Who is in charge?' - no answer
3. Chinese say 'yes' or 'no'	Japanese say 'maybe'

Westerners who are used to being given a job and left to get on with it do not always take kindly to being members of the 'company family'. Consequently, when their Japanese seniors in the West question them on how they are going to do a job, and production and quality control specialists are sent to assist them, it does not always meet with their approval, even if the visitors insist: 'We're from head office, we're here to help you!' But to the Japanese its all part of an integrated team effort. They also prefer cross-craft skills for simple maintenance work rather than demarcation. Likewise, with the right attitudes to teamwork, if a job needs to be completed, everyone stays late in the office or factory until it's finished.

In the West competitiveness is valued, and the cult of

individualism has prevailed still more in recent years. Japanese-style team work and loyalty frequently appear to Caucasians as regimentation or even indoctrination. Whereas a Japanese maintains he owes his company a great deal for providing lifetime employment, the average Westerner will tell you he owes his employer little, and he himself has contributed his skills and talent, and, consequently, both parties have benefitted. That is why, in Japanese enterprises in the West, they try not to overdo or force the spirit of loyalty.

Chapter 12
Communications

Because dialogue is essential if a partnership between management and workers is to be effective, emphasis should be placed on clear cut objectives and close and continual communications in both directions. That is why on some Japanese managers' doors you see the sign, PLEASE DO DISTURB!, and why some senior managers like to give a weekly address to their company although this is not mandatory. Certainly, if a partnership is to work, the partners have to talk to one another and there has to be mutual understanding.

In the 1970s, a British association, the Industrial Society, which provides training and advice on industrial relations and personnel management, advocated openness of information, and that workers should be told what is happening in their firms. Surely in any organisation, even if eastern and western cultures are different, that seems perfectly natural?

Many Japanese firms go to lengths, for instance in their workers' handbooks, to point out that everyone will be given a say in how best to do his or her job and how to improve the working environment. In a Japanese company the normal way to commence work is for a group, together with a manager or a foreman, to discuss the previous day's production, and attempt to anticipate problems. Employees may also recite a slogan at the start and at the end of each shift, such as:

A LITTLE BETTER EVERY DAY.

Or perhaps they pledge to work conscientiously and

amicably together. Although the Westerner may exclaim, 'Oh dear: we grew out of that sort of thing years ago!' In the case of the Japanese, and some other nationalities, it really does work.

Another important channel for communications is the company's advisory council which meets, say, once a month. This is composed of senior managers and ten or twelve elected representatives — often union members — from various divisions of the enterprise. Subjects discussed include present activities, problems, policies, future plans, safety, welfare, salaries and other relevant topics.

The Japanese see meetings as fact finding sessions. Among themselves, within their own culture with its accompanying nuances, they normally know what conclusions have been decided. But often in overseas Japanese firms, because of an absence of straight talking as they try not to offend, it is not always possible for an American or a European to understand what they are thinking or what is intended.

Because of tacit understanding, what amounts to codified social interaction, and the importance of unspoken language, the Japanese, as we have seen, often have difficulty in communicating with the outside world. Indeed sometimes they misunderstand each other. In Japanese it is rude to say 'no'. Although 'yes' and 'no' are the oldest and simplest of words they require the most thought in use. To be polite in Japanese you have to be evasive, and a direct refusal is therefore to be avoided. If the reply is, 'I shall do what I can', or 'I shall think about it', you need to be able to sense a person's unwillingness or inability to do something. What he is usually trying to tell you is NO! It's a nicer way of putting it.

For instance a Chinese secretary several years ago who

wanted to change jobs, in order to give her European boss 'face', told him she was going overseas to further her studies; whereas, in reality, she was moving because of better pay and job prospects. Some embarrassment was caused a few weeks later when she met her old boss in the street! But to her, to tell a 'white lie' was permissible. It was more important to give face.

Chapter 13
Human Relations

One of the main areas where the West can learn from the East is in labour-management relations, where the basis of relationships is, as we have seen, interdependence and trust. Confucius lauded 'The Great Harmony', sometimes known as the *Wa Spirit* (pronounced *woh* in Cantonese and meaning, in harmony, peaceful, together), where everyone knew his or her place.

Considerable effort is made in the average company to promote a non-confrontational ambience and to treat employees well. Because Japanese and Chinese managers know that no matter how capable an employee is he can wreck the atmosphere on the factory floor, more importance is placed on attitudes than on skills when recruiting.

The main aim of the small Chinese firm, named say Loyalty and Company, where ownership (shareholding) overlaps with control (managing), is to make a profit. It is task oriented and managers know that without a surplus the company cannot survive. But this is not its only objective. The 'Old World' (boss) realises the importance, especially in a climate of low unemployment, of treating employees well. 'The sovereign should rule benevolently and the subjects are required to be loyal: the father should show his love for his sons who are obliged to display filial piety' (from one of *The Four Books, The Great Learning*, containing the words, conversations and opinions of Confucius [551-479 BC] as recorded by his disciples). Reciprocity and harmony are important parts of the Confucian heritage and Chinese cultural legacy. An employer should display deep commitment to his workforce through paternalistic welfare capitalism.

Most Chinese, Japanese and Korean businesses adopt a policy of utilitarianistic paternalism, with its obligatory authority, relationships, hierarchical status, organisational roles and functions. These bonds, cemented by unity, harmony, loyalty and emotional commitment, are considered important. In the Chinese case the patriarchal ideology requires the father figure to take a personal interest in all his employees. In showing concern and benevolence he knows there will be mutual benefits. His staff are considered to be assets and special, and, in everything other than the strict legal sense, as his people. Many bosses may be seen daily in close interaction with their workers and visit them when they are sick.

Within the company ethos, with cohesive kinship bonds and altrustic obligations, employees accept their social identity and positions as members of their industrial family. They have a sense of belonging and feel secure within their work culture. They co-operate by safeguarding, as far as positions allow, the interests of the owner-manager, and they perform their tasks to the best of their ability. In the traditions of Chinese virtue the workers offer their patriarch loyalty.

Lee Kuan Yew has been quoted as an example of benevolent paternalism. He, and his board of directors, the Government, provide leadership and protection to the citizens of Singapore like an extended family and, in return, Lee expects people to be industrious and to save (it is compulsory to contribute to the Central Provident Fund). The aim is to develop a sense of belonging, and a bright future is proffered if citizens do as they are told. But woe be unto him or her who does not obey the patriarch! There are advantages. Although some Westerners consider such a system outdated, even Winston Churchill is purported to have said the most efficient form of government is a benevolent dictatorship.

There are natural variations, and Douglas McGregor, the American, opened up a whole new human-relations avenue in the 1950s when he coined the term 'Theory X' for authoritarian leadership where the assumption is that humans dislike work and most are not ambitious. It is assumed that employees have to be controlled and motivation is brought about by physiological needs, security and money.

The alternative, McGregor said, is 'Theory Y', namely participatory or democratic management, where workers largely supervise themselves and have a voice in advancing the job and goals of the organisation. With Theory Y work is considered 'as natural as play', and if conditions are favourable and people are properly motivated, they can be creative and self-directed. The aim is for workers to become self-actualised (as jargon has it), and the leader of a team has been likened to the conductor of an orchestra.

Under the right circumstances, with a less educated and more dependent group which requires positive leadership, Theory X can be effective and can produce high morale. The Old China, as one would perhaps expect, normally employed Theory X, as does much of the People's Republic today.

It is surprising how, when walking through a factory or office, one is soon able to sense the atmosphere. This was brought home to the writer when he, together with a group of management students, visited a car plant in the south of England in 1964. Managers smartly dressed, with

jackets and ties, were jeered by the workers in their over-
alls on the shop floor. Not long afterwards they came out
on strike.

A similar thing happened during a training course for
the National Coal Board in 1972. On a trip down a pit in
Yorkshire aimed at obtaining a better idea of what it was
like at the coal face, it was apparent then that a strong
movement was building up against the management.
Industrial action started not long afterwards.

These examples contrast with that of Starlite Printers
Limited, employing over 200 staff in Hong Kong, who
produce packaging materials, books, magazines and novel-
ties. The firm was established in 1972 by K.Y. Lam, a
Hakka Chinese who came to Hong Kong in 1963 from
Guangdong Province in China. Today, much of his time
is spent walking around his factory talking to employees
in a warm and supportive way. The message that comes
across is, 'We're all in this together like a family.' This is
observable on visiting his works or attending company
functions such as anniversaries, and annual and spring
dinners. The company objective, to excel and strive for
perfection, has paid off. Lam was one of the recipients of
the Federation of Hong Kong Industries '1988 Young
Industrialist's Awards'. Modestly, Lam insists that his
business successes are due to luck. However, it seems that
the harder he works the luckier he becomes.

But success is a two-way process, and the firm has
made generous donations to the community and provided
assistance to worthy causes. Although the company is not
large, emphasis is placed on training and attendance at
seminars. Also, the staff go overseas for a group holiday
every year which is largely paid for by the firm.

Similarly, the late H.C. Ting believed in running his

factory — Kader (Hong Kong) which manufactures plastic items — on paternalistic lines. In his book, 'Truth and Facts', he quotes the Chinese proverb, "It's easy to set up a shop but it is far more difficult to set up a staff." As he says, "... one must learn to know ... everything about your (sic) men — their individual capabilities, honesty, industriousness etc. (and) to know how (they will) behave under a particular set of circumstances." He goes on to say that one must know how to reward and penalise them effectively, be fair at all times, and set an example. Ting warns, however, of the danger of being 'over-indulgent to staff' which can lead to slackness. 'It is not always possible to satisfy everybody, but seek, without fail, to satisfy your conscience.'

It has been emphasised that relations should go beyond office doors or factory gates, and work groups in Japan seem to delight in hitting the town, drinking, and having a singsong together. *Karaoke* halls, on Japanese lines, are now common in the Far East, where a wide variety of taped music can be requested and the words of songs, coupled with a story in pictures, is flashed, hi-tech fashion, on to television screens. The group sings in unison, but, at times, individuals are expected to perform, solo, accompanied by applause and some bantering. A few firms in Hong Kong, such as Standard-Chartered Bank have set up their own *Karaoke* equipment for staff use. A singsong is usually preceded by a meal together.

Large Japanese corporations have gone just about as far as is possible with regard to all-embracing concern and welfare (*Kikubari*). Among other benefits they often provide housing, medical care, packaged holidays, and long-service premiums. A few even maintain space in temples for the ashes of deceased employees so a company's

61

'cohesiveness' and 'spirit' is carried into the next world. Staff work, play and pray together.

Although the last practice would be unthinkable in the West, when borrowing from Japan, 'overcoming "them and us" with one family reality' has been cited by Charles Villiers in his book, 'Start Again Britain', as a main area where action is needed. Many workers in Japanese factories in America and Europe will tell you: 'This is the best place I've ever worked. Others will say, 'They know what they're about and make us feel like a family', or similar words. This shows that Japanese methods of creating harmony can be successful when modified to suit western environments.

However, when this is not done properly, understandably, problems arise. Examples exist, in Japanese factories in Germany, where Japanese-style management has not been 'blended' into the local culture and is therefore not popular. Likewise, many Hong Kong Chinese workers prefer to work for an American firm rather than for an old foe, the Japanese, and those Hongkongers that do take up employment with the latter are often criticised by the Japanese for their high turnover rate and lack of loyalty.

Many, nonetheless, believe Japan's ascendancy to world economic superpower status has been largely the result of an overall concern for people, and a superior concept of human relationships which are both subtle and powerful even if the Japanese lifestyle has limited appeal to many nationalities. Because only its employees can make a firm successful, a Japanese manager spends much of his time trying to build healthy human relationships, a corporate spirit, and a shared sense of fate which help to bind staff and company together. (The term *onjo-shugi* means an understanding and sympathetic boss.)

Some of the most revealing research, which illustrates the importance of human relations in the West, are the 'ageless' Hawthorne experiments. These were conducted by Elton Mayo, a clinical psychologist at Harvard Business School, from 1924 to 1927, largely in the wiring rooms of Western Electric's plant at Hawthorne, New Jersey, in the United States. A great deal of data were obtained and interpretations are still being made. But the main conclusion that emerged was that paying regard to employees is well worth while. When one female operative was asked, in a workshop at Hawthorne, why her section had done so well and production had gone up in spite of worse working conditions she replied : **'We were made to feel we were important; We mattered!'**

Did they really need these tests, you may ask, when such a conclusion must be obvious to any intelligent manager? The answer is, 'probably not!' But the way some firms are run, one would not think managers are aware of the need for sound personnel-management tenets.

Yes, a lot of research has been conducted in the West, but the Japanese have applied human-relations principles in industry to a greater extent and taken them further. Although Britain has been able to motivate its managers successfully, the Japanese have been able to inspire their entire workforce.

Chapter 14
Management Grids

Figure 1: Blake's management grid

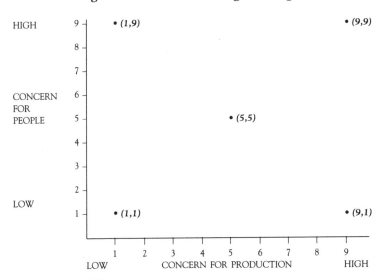

- **1,1 MANAGEMENT**
  Direction of minimum effort to get required work done and to sustain 'membership' of organisation (Impoverished management)
- **1,9 MANAGEMENT**
  Thoughtful attention to needs of people for satisfying relationships leads to a comfortable, friendly, organisational atmosphere and work tempo (Country Club management)
- **5,5 MANAGEMENT**
  Adequate performance is possible through balancing the necessity to get work done with maintaining morale of people at a satisfactory level (Middle-of-the-road management)
- **9,1 MANAGEMENT**
  Efficiency in operations results from arranging conditions of work in such a way that human elements interfere to a minimum degree (Task management)
- **9,9 MANAGEMENT**
  (most effective) Work accomplished by committed people, inter-dependence through a 'common stake' in organisational purpose leads to relationships of trust and respect (Team management)

Various methods have been used to try to measure management styles, and one example, as shown at Figure 1, is the grid which was devised by Robert R. Blake and Jane S. Mouton. The vertical axis relates to 'concern for people', while the horizontal axis measures 'concern for production'. The extreme readings on this grid are : 1/9 nicknamed 'country-club management', 1/1 'impoverished management', 9/1 'task management', and 9/9 (the most effective) which is 'team management'. A firm which is awarded half marks for both 'concern for people' and 'concern for production' is thus a 5/5 or middle of the road company. Most Japanese companies seem to do well on both counts.

Chapter 15
Personnel Relations —
What can the West learn?

In the West, the tendency has been to divorce personal feelings and sentiment from management operations and worker control for fear of losing objectivity. But even in Europe paternalism is by no means unknown. Examples which exist — or existed until fairly recently — include those at Michelin at Clermont-Ferrand in France, Krupp at Essen in Germany, and Fiat in Italy. In England, the Cadbury organisation at Bournville and Lever Brothers at Port Sunlight, with their model villages and staff amenities, are well known. Up to World War II in Europe apprentices, too, were often treated in paternalistic ways, and workers, for example dressmakers, frequently lived in accommodation above their shops. Other western firms that have prided themselves on outstanding relations with their staff include Mercedes-Benz, Volkswagon, Siemens and Bata shoe company. Even IBM was built up using good, old-fashioned, people-oriented, precepts.

Western entrepreneurs who ran — and in a few cases still run — their firms on the above lines are now commonly regarded with a certain amount of cynicism. Many critics go so far as to say their personal attention and moralising are objectionable and a fraudulent cover for enhancing profits.

Certainly in the East — and possibly in the West too-much criticism is often unfair. Nevertheless, in the latter there has been a shift away from such practices and paternalism has usually been dropped altogether. In many cases, the aim has been, with objectivity in mind, to dehumanise the workplace. Paternalism has thus often been construed as exploitation and a remnant of feudal times, although it is believed by some that two long-established family firms, Marks and Spencer, and J. Sainsbury Ltd, weathered the mid-1970s oil crisis and recession in Britain better than most companies due largely to a combination of sound financial control and benign paternalism. John Lewis also has a good record. But so often the West sees paternalism as condescending, patronising, and as treating employees as if they are immature.

Yet the above methods are still a way of life in the East, and Asians believe paternalism is inherently superior to impersonal western ways of handling people. The oriental view is of each person as a unique individual, and one needs to be a different type of manager to look at employees in this way. Harmony, compassion and empathy are required if one wants to get the best out of him or her. The Asian method is more personalised and humanistic. Also in the NIEs, with their low unemployment rates, the recruiting and training of skilled personnel is often difficult and expensive, and, having made an investment in people, an effort must be made to retain them. In any case, there is a distinct difference between out of date Victorian paternalism and the shared, committed fate, and egalitarian system, that is in vogue in Japan today.

With the adoption of more high technology in the Asian NIEs, and as more firms become partially westernised, there will be a greater commitment to modern management. But it is hoped the responsibility of enterprises towards people will not be unduly affected, and as a result paternalism will remain an important and effective part of business. There is no need to drop it. It serves a useful purpose in the Asian setting. Firms can accept significant involvement embracing both paternalism and high technology. But although the former is deeply ingrained it is probable, as people in the East become better educated and more influenced by the West, that they too may construe paternalism as being condescending. Its influence therefore is likely to diminish with time. Management in the East will become less personal, and will be based less on intuition and the personality of the executive. Greater emphasis will be put on the rational systems approach.

But in spite of what we read about firms in the East being run harmoniously it is not always like that. Although Chinese and Japanese are seen by the uninformed Westerner as 'inscrutable' they can be emotional people who hide their feelings in what can be very competitive societies. The Chinese have been described as 'thermos flasks', cold on the outside and hot inside. Those who have worked in, or with, Chinese or Japanese organisations know that not infrequently staff relations are not 'sweet', and interactions do not always run smoothly. Nevertheless, generally, more effort is made with human resources in the Far East than in the West, and this pays off. And so the next lesson, in keeping with a message to workers on a factory wall in Japan, is:

MOVE FORWARD IN HARMONY
WITH THE WORLD.

Indeed the Japanese system of personnel relations is now one of the most successful ways in which management and employees can jointly profit from their endeavours. Such methods, together with bottom-up management, joint decision making, and the involvement of human resources at all levels, can create an environment where there are fewer barriers to the introduction of new technology and change.

Chapter 16
Laws and Regulations

Asians, tend to be less litigious than most Westerners. A large amount of business is discussed in Chinese tea houses. Deals are 'sealed by the lips' and little is committed to paper. Offshore Chinese, as well as Koreans, are not in favour of elaborate written contracts. Japanese firms do not normally use them either among themselves, although, because this may sound disturbing to a Westerner, they are employed when coming to an agreement with foreign companies, 'Because', as one Japanese put it, 'You people like to have everything set down in writing.'

This 'mutual understanding', which Japanese, Koreans, and Chinese rely upon among their own people, is often implicit. They argue any contract is only as effective as the willingness of the concerned parties to execute. If something goes wrong the best answer is to discuss it. It has been said the Japanese have so few lawsuits because of their desire for consensus. This tradition stretches back to the rice paddies of ancient *Yamato* the legendary birthplace of Japanese culture and the nation.

Similarly the Chinese, with their Confucian backgrounds and principles of *Li* (propriety), do not need to resort to formal laws and regulations. Informal rules, which to them are equally binding, replace what could otherwise be cumbersome, impersonal, bureaucratic machinery. In any case, it is not easy to draft a contract in Japanese which, if it is not to cause offence, has to be in indirect language.

The average East Asian businessman is honest,

trustworthy, sympathetic and generous, and, for example because of the lack or brevity of written agreements, an architect will expect a contractor to solve problems on site if humanly possible. Only when no other solution can be found do Asians resort to law. They dislike having to employ lawyers and prefer to settle disputes by negotiation, bargaining, and by mediation out of court.

There are over 600,000 lawyers in the United States (280 per 100,000 of the population), more than 64,000 in Britain (115), and only just over 13,000 (11) in Japan. Japanese lawyers also enjoy less social status and poorer career opportunities than their United States counterparts. Some businessmen joke and say America has ten lawyers for one engineer while Japan has ten engineers for every lawyer.

Chapter 17
Connections

So-called 'networks' are less clearly defined than hierarchies. They are not just sentimental ties. To a degree, in the East they substitute for the laws and legal systems of the West. Instead of signing a contract — a mere piece of paper — time, effort and money are expended building up and earning trust and endeavouring to 'belong'. Business, they believe, cannot be conducted in a vacuum. Even *Lo Baak Sing* ('Old 100 Names', in Chinese meaning the common man) knows that without connections it is risky to conduct any transaction, and that it is important to honour reciprocal trust. A second set of standards exists for the outsider.

In 1989, Japanese firms spent US$32 billion, or what amounted to an average of US$17,300 in entertainment expenses for every Japanese firm. These are tax deductible. Costly gifts are also given to curry favours and the line dividing generous Asian hospitality and outright bribery is not always easy to discern.

It was explained that you have to work at it: 'If you haven't developed a good network of relationships by the age of thirty-five you're in trouble. They need to be cultivated well before you actually need them.' As elsewhere, it is often useful to know someone who knows somebody else, and an Asian entrepreneur will go to great lengths to cultivate connections, often with a specific end in view. On numerous occasions the author has been openly asked by Chinese colleagues and acquaintances, who wanted something done, if he knew anybody in such and such an organisation. Many Chinese bosses also do not tackle problems head on. They get around them by getting to know persons in the right places who could help. Sometimes one can have difficulty in obtaining information from Japanese firms because one does not know anyone in an influential position.

Business is more personal in the Orient, instead of a system of rights and obligations with rigid boundaries created by laws and lawyers. However in Hong Kong and Singapore, with their colonial traditions, 'networking' is combined with a British style legal systems and a sense of order. The latter is not so obvious in Taiwan.

The Japanese and Chinese make friends first, build up dependency and trust, and then do business later. These friendship ties extend to customers, subcontractors, suppliers and other associates. Such connections are stronger with the Japanese who will stay with one loyal supplier or subcontractor, who forms part of the team, whereas the Chinese may shop around to find the best prices. Japanese in the West often complain about suppliers and subcontractors for their poor quality products and late delivery. In Japan they are called in, they have dinner together, and they work to sort things out.

Japanese networks depend on a corporate environment, broad intergroup linkages, and power of office. 'Which company does he belong to?' and 'What post does he hold?', are common questions. Within the web of business and community of firms social factors within the institutional framework, and connections with government officials are important. Communications can be vertical, horizontal, national or global, with a wide range of variations. In Singapore, for example, business groups are organised around the non-nationalised banks.

But blood is thicker than water and strong links exist among Chinese family members. Often nobody else is relied upon to keep his or her hand out of the till. Positions of trust in Chinese family firms are frequently barred to outsiders, and, in hard times, relatives will work for food, shelter and psychological support. Any problem in the family stays within the family. In addition to the hierarchy of kinship (based on generation, age, sex etc.), clan, i.e., sharing a common surname, and originating from the same native place in China are important. You do not engage an unfamiliar person to work for you unless he can be vouched for by someone in your network. Because it is often difficult to find people with the right qualifications many firms remain small. But, when family and business intertwine, human emotions often become magnified and an outsider is sometimes puzzled as to what extent nepotism can work effectively.

Certainly networks, which separate members from non-members, exist in most societies in some form; like the 'old school tie' in England. The author remembers one of his firm's regular suppliers — a wholesale ironmonger in Britain — whose grandfather had done business with his grandfather and great-grandfather. But connections are more important in the East and one can learn from them.

Nepotism has, in fact, been practised in many European companies in the Orient. In *The Thistle and the Jade*, a book about the famous British business house Jardine Matheson, Alan Reid, one of the nine co-authors, says:

"... for over a century one family and its collateral branches have been chiefly concerned in the overall management, success and future of the firm. It .sounds like nepotism, but nepotism of a shrewd, discriminating kind, devised and set in motion at a time when family obligations came high on the list."

Is nepotism one of the secrets of success and longevity of Jardines and other organisations out East?

In recent years in the West we have come to appreciate that systems and rationality are not the only components that make transactions run smoothly. Today, quite rightly, more emphasis is placed on co-operation and collaboration. Yet as far back as the 1920s Mary Parker Follett, the American industrial psychologist and advocate of harmonious human relations, was stressing the importance of informal communications.

Nevertheless it would be wrong to overestimate the value of *quanxi* (Chinese networking). It certainly cannot guarantee success. One criticism is that it is too person centred. Also, more research is needed to ascertain the optimum market structure with the right combination of co-operation and competitiveness. Good examples are the Cantonese and Shanghainese businessmen in Hong Kong with their combination of networking and competition. The Korean *chaebols* co-operate to a more limited degree.

Chapter 18
Trade Unions

In Japan unions are generally of the single, in-house type, and both white and blue-collar workers, who all draw monthly salaries and are 'one great middle class', are members. Although the factory floor is not always serene, and unions are by no means invariably subservient, there is not the British 19th century 'smokestack' tradition of conflict, and Japanese 'honourable management' and workers have a reputation for concessions, co-operation and compromise. In the same way that the West had its Protestant work ethic, so the East has its Buddhist and Confucian philosophies and a high degree of commitment and reluctance to strike.

This is not to be confused with Singapore, which has a good labour relations record, but whose workers have no right to strike. There, disputes are referred to the Ministry of Labour for mediation and conciliation.

In Japan, unions tend not to be looked upon by managers as an alien force but rather as providing peaceful competition in an altruistic, unitary, business world. They regularly meet management, not just to negotiate and bargain, but as social partners to discuss such topics as how employees can obtain greater job satisfaction. They can, nonetheless, fight hard to ensure nobody is sacked.

Partly no doubt because of their life-time employment policy there is not the same negative attitudes towards robots and other advanced technology as is often witnessed in the West. The former are seen as valuable and reliable helpmates which relieve humans of dirty, dangerous, mundane tasks. This acceptance of technology by the public and the workforce is another strength of the Japanese. Employees seem to be more psychologically prepared for this, partly because they have a say in the running of their firm.

Some Westerners ask why the Japanese choose to establish factories in Britain, with its poor record of unrest and abrasive, obstreperous attitudes of workers. To be fair, industrial relations have improved a great deal in the United Kingdom in recent years. Nevertheless, one of the main advantages that the Japanese have is, because they are foreigners there, they have been able to introduce single-union agreements and management styles which might have been banned by the labour force if implemented by indigenous companies. Nonetheless, one Japanese firm in Britain did try to form its own in-house labour union but this was not allowed to operate by other unions.

What has actually emerged is a compromise between typical western trade unions and Japanese in-house (company) unions. Consequently, although an agreement may not explicitly express a no-strike clause, it implies it. This is done by incorporating binding arbitration provisions and the setting up of some form of works council. Toshiba, in Britain, is an example.

By contrast, a western firm, on establishing a business in Tokyo, was offered a no-strike agreement by its workers who were amazed when it was refused by the British management on the grounds it was not democratic.

To some extent, Japanese firms in the West have been successful in avoiding adversarial attitudes and confrontational politics. This has been possible largely because their methods are seen, generally, as not being authoritarian.

Indeed their open management style, with employees encouraged to participate in various ways in the running of a company, has been popular with unions outside Japan. They also try to take a long-term view — which can be construed as an antidote for western inertia — and although they may not have a policy in the West of lifetime employment, the Japanese (to their credit) try to avoid layoffs. Working conditions and concern for welfare also rank high. Hence, it is not surprising that Japanese firms in the West have a better industrial relations record than most local businesses.

But probably at the root of their success is the basic philosophy: A UNION IS NOT THERE TO CREATE CONFRONTATION BUT TO AVOID IT AND ITS PURPOSE IS TO ASSIST MANAGEMENT WITH THE RUNNING OF A COMPANY.

Chapter 19
The Shop Floor

With the emphasis on flexibility, the Japanese on an assembly line function in small, efficient groups. Working alongside such personnel, identified by inconspicious badges on their company uniforms, are the foremen, other supervisory staff and people like shop stewards. Together they undertake fire-fighting, and deal with on-the-job problems as they arise, at their discretion. Although the Japanese are being undercut in price by leaner and meaner manufacturers in places like South Korea and Taiwan, nevertheless they have generally learned to make good quality products more cheaply and efficiently than anyone else. They combine low-cost operations with the highest productivity to maintain their competitive edge.

3913 kamikaze ('suicide') pilots died in midget torpedoes, in aeroplanes (often over loaded with extra fuel) or in Ohka rocket bombs, in the Second World War, and Westerners sometimes lament that this old samurai warrior caste spirit is carried over into industry. Just as during World War II no officers of the equivalent rank of major or above surrendered until instructed to do so by Emperor Hirohito in 1945, so there is seemingly total dedication at work. No one speaks or smokes on the assembly line. There are ten-minute breaks to allow employees to go to the lavatory. One instructor in Japan told his charges: **"Every ten minutes spent working should be lived as if it is the last ten minutes of your lives. If you don't enjoy your work you are wasting your time."**

As always, tremendous attention is paid to detail. The

author learned Karate in the Far East, and, after obtaining a Black Belt, became an instructor. The class was made to repeat endlessly, year after year, the most simple basic movements, kicks and strikes. Although Westerners joke and say there are three methods for doing anything, the right way, the wrong way, and the Japanese way, they have a special term, *Kaizen*, for seeking to do a job more efficiently. Like learning Karate movements, tasks are standardised at the workplace. People are not taught *how* to think but *what* to think. A great deal of rote learning, as is required to master the difficult Japanese and Chinese languages, more so than for learning European languages, pervades education and training as a whole. Attempts are made to teach simple, standard answers to complex questions.

On the assembly line, workers are expected to accomplish a movement in exactly the same way — the one 'correct' way — every time. A wide variety of techniques are employed to reduce waste and to provide flexibility in order to update products quickly and cheaply. Another byword they have learned is:

TO BE ABLE TO MAKE PRODUCTS FLEXIBLY
YOU MUST FIRST MAKE THEM SIMPLE.

Laying down plain, quality, performance standards in engineering design and production, such as the common man can understand, has been another secret of their success.

The Japanese develop new cars in under four years, twice as fast as most western manufacturers, although this quest for speed has occasionally meant sacrificing allied activities, such as in-depth market research. Correctly or incorrectly they have even occasionally been accused of rushing ill-conceived ideas on to the market. Neverthe-

82

less, in Japan where concentration is on applied, rather than pure, research, research and development (R&D) has mostly paid its way, unlike in a number of countries where much has been government sponsored.

In spite of what has been suggested considerable attention is paid to market research, and a single universal product may be replaced by a range targeted for different countries depending upon the preferences of the inhabitants. For example, Japanese television sets are made with artificial timber veneer specially to suit the preference of the British. There is now a move towards bespoke car making and even door-to-door car salesmen in Japan.

Many Japanese complain that Westerners have too narrow a concept of quality and that this should extend to a broader view embracing marketing and customer service and satisfaction. One of the first lessons the Japanese trainee learns is 'the customer is always right', and after-sales service can reach almost religious proportions. Their view is different to many Chinese establishments which believe that once goods have changed hands the deal has been consummated.

Of course conditions vary from one Japanese factory to another. Some managers are required to spend half an hour on the production line daily, not just for humility or as a penance but to keep in touch with the shop floor. A senior Japanese manager in the United States is said to spend nearly as much time in the factory as in his office. There is a story of one who, as he does his rounds, frequently picks up pieces of paper. (In a Japanese company everyone is responsible for cleanliness.) He may also be seen rolling up the sleeves of his company uniform and, when necessary, working long into the night. These actions have endeared him to his subordinates who he prefers to call colleagues. This manager's watchword is:

ORDERLINESS AND CLEANILESS

MAKE QUALITY.

However, a German professor has said:

"We Germans are very production oriented. If we are on the factory floor or in the office we work hard. The Japanese may stay late because they want to be seen to be there, but they often don't achieve much."

In Japan they are termed *gozensama*, or 'Mr Morning', because they leave home early and return late at night. Others are called *tanshin funin* or 'business bachelors'. Correctly or incorrectly *karoshi* (death from overwork) has long been given as the reason for a series of fatalities among business heads, including top managers of a big robotics company, a large publishing firm and a communications organisation. Although the Japanese Government refuses to use the term *karoshi*, it has in recent years been urging managers to take more time off.

Another success story is that of Komatsu, which makes earth-moving equipment at County Durham in the north of England. This firm has won the appreciation of its employees by the team-work and support provided. Yet some workers in a Japanese factory in the United States, to give another side to the picture, said that the basic characteristics and requirements of Americans, who are more demanding and individualistic than the Japanese, are sometimes ignored.

You cannot, of course, please everyone, but there are countless cases where the Japanese have done their best to make provisions for corporate culture overseas, and on some production lines in Wales allowances are made for workers who would rather stand than sit as is the custom in Japan.

It has been reported that Japanese managers in the West show great sensitivity to production line employees, but they are frequently not so effective when it comes to managing other functions. This is one point of view. However, results achieved by the Japanese in their business ventures seem to prove otherwise.

Material for a good case study, showing how Japanese methods were able to turn a car plant into another profitable project, could be obtained from New United Motor Manufacturing, at Fremont California. A joint venture between General Motors and Toyota, the plant re-opened in 1983. It was run by General Motors until it closed in 1982, and was described as a battle ground between management and labour with wildcat strikes.

Eighty-five per cent of the original workforce were re-employed, absenteeism was reduced from 20 to 4 per cent, the productivity of the old plant was doubled, and the new plant, it has been claimed, is 50 per cent more efficient than its all-American counterpart factories. The important factor that brought about the startling improvements is, in essence, a revitalised corporate culture. Sweeping management changes have included giving workers some responsibility for production and avoiding laying them off.

Other old standby that can usually be relied upon to achieve a favourable outcome including doing away with reserved parking spaces and segregated dining rooms have been employed, although morning exercises, uniforms and company songs are not the order of the day at New United Motor Manufacturing Company. One of the main reasons for the improvements was greater recognition and consideration for workers on the assembly line. Coupled with this has been job rotation, to provide job enrichment and enhance workers' skills, a well laid out shop floor and an obsession with orderliness and cleanliness. Considerable attention is paid to the timing of delivery of parts, and 'networks' with suppliers and subcontractors. The above has been coupled with high technical competence and involvement by Japanese management which has enabled it to be accepted on the shop floor. A firm that has different, competing, corporate cultures, one for shopfloor workers, another for management and so on, finds them pulling in different directions. Now that has changed.

Today, salaries are among the highest in the industry and employees seem satisfied working under Japanese management. Nonetheless, a few complain about the speed of the assembly line which makes it difficult for older members to keep up. It remains to be seen in such overseas factories if enthusiasm and sense of responsibility will continue when the pressure is on. For example, at New United Motor Manufacturing Incorporated, some American designed cars have not sold well and production has had to be cut.

The pure Japanese approach is an amalgam of dedication, loyalty and uniformity. Although the aim is to keep the production process simple, there can be a pernickety Japanese fixation with detail and what would be considered in the West as ruthless employment practices. These include a constant unrelenting, search for improvements in speed and quality, and strict discipline, although much of this is self-imposed.

Whether in the East or the West there is normally more than adequate Japanese investment in equipment. Although tariff barriers in the home country can be high, they prefer to buy the best, discounting whether it is manufactured in Japan or elsewhere. The Japanese do not suffer, as one English engineer put it, from the 'not made in Japan rejection syndrome.'

The assembly line turns slowly in the early months after a new product is introduced, and speed is increased as operatives become more proficient. In Japan, with their sense of teamwork, fast workers help their colleagues when they fall behind or feel off colour. At the same time, quality is top priority and, if necessary, the assembly line is stopped to ensure defective products do not reach the market.

Some workers in Japanese factories in the United States, when they have found the going too tough, have objected in subtle, unobtrusive ways — such as by not doing morning exercises, not attending after-work meetings or by not using their initiative and putting forward suggestions. As is to be expected not all methods in Japanese factories meet with the approval of every Westerner.

Chapter 20
Quality Circles and Suggestion Schemes

An aid to team building and a way for management to upgrade standards is by forming 'quality control circles' (QCs). A group of 10 or 12 acquainted workers from the same field, often under their foreman, meet perhaps once a week on a voluntary but usually paid basis for one hour. Under their trained leader the group discusses or brain-storms anything concerning day-to-day working arrangements, smoother operations, quality control and related problems. The Japanese believe it is better to anticipate complications and prevent defects than to have to correct them, and all staff are encouraged to make suggestions. These can range from a remedy for a weak seal on an engine to improved methods of production or working conditions or an aspect of safety or plant tidiness. Each group is expected to come up with from four to eight suggestions a month. One motto is:

CONSTANTLY SEARCH FOR A BETTER WAY.

QCs have, however, been described as too task-oriented and neglecting human factors, although these, too, can be subjects for discussion.

Incidentally, quality circles, which are usually thought of as being typically Japanese, were introduced there from the United States. They have since proved effective and popular in Japan, although they have never caught on in America and Europe to the same extent. Circles are also employed, to varying degrees, in the four Asian NIEs where they are more common in South Korea and Taiwan. QCs have not become so popular in Hong Kong although there is a quality control circle association there. Reasons given are along the lines of firms generally being small with high labour turnover, many workers not being well educated and having no real sense of belonging, and enterprise and management not being receptive to the idea. QCs have been formed, however, by the Hong Kong and Shanghai Banking Corporation where they are known as 'Work Improvement Teams' (WITs). Bank staff have assured the author that such teams have been useful in this non-manufacturing environment. Neither are QCs common in Singapore except in Japanese firms based there.

The Japanese, with their penchant for co-operation, have been able to make significant use of quality circles. This is partly because, with their rigid hierarchy, juniors are not, under normal circumstances, expected to contradict superiors. As mentioned earlier they do, however, have their own ways, built into the system, of voicing opinions, such as joint decision making, bottom-up management and quality circles, even if views are required to be expressed in a respectful and formal manner.

In the land where lifelong employment is still common many suggestions made by personnel at the work place can be valuable, and if the firm prospers and later pays higher wages everyone benefits in the longer term. Despite some language barriers in the early stages of overseas plants Japanese managements, with their basic bottom-up style, have consistently made it clear that they expect to hear from employees at all levels although, obviously, not all suggestions are implemented.

In America and Europe employees do not always see things in that light, and Japanese overseas have often been disappointed at the number and quality of suggestions received from western workers. Many are prepared just to do their jobs and are not keen to make extra voluntary effort.'That's the manager's job,' they believe. When working for a typical western firm employees are not expected to take too much initiative, and that is one of the reasons why, in a Japanese firm which uses quality circles, workers may not fulfil the expectations of management. Western junior managers, too, may feel their authority is being usurped.

A quiet introduction of quality circles is likely to be the best tactic, possibly on a pilot-scheme basis but with a clear understanding that they are fully supported by management and all ideas and proposals will be considered. The timing of their introduction, which needs appropriate publicity, must be examined carefully and their purpose explained. It would not, for instance, be done at the time a redundancy programme was being put into effect or a major restructuring of the company was taking place. To promote a spirit of harmony, trade union representatives should be involved. The British Trades Union Congress has made it clear, although they support the idea of quality circles, that these will be opposed if they conflict with union practices. For the circles to function as intended, members need instruction and assistance from trained 'facilitators', and there should be feedback regarding the effectiveness of circles.

Some Japanese companies which believe in giving rewards have a points system for suggestions — which may be displayed on the canteen wall — and individuals or groups are recompensed in cash or in kind. By making a suggestion that is implemented, all team members may earn points which entitle them to choose from a list of prizes that include, say, a towel, a pair of socks, a corkscrew, or an overseas group holiday.

It requires time and effort to make QCs work in an occidental culture, where established principles of individuals offering competing ideas may militate against group solutions. But if the employee believes he or she is not just working for the company (with its policy of long-term employment), but in effect for him or herself, then it will be easier to keep the enthusiasm and momentum of quality circles going. Workers must be made to feel that their ideas are respected, and that they, as important people in the company, are participating in policy making. Experience has shown that quality circles can reap dividends in the West providing a company pays regard to experience gained in other countries. They should not be imposed on staff without regard to their feelings, and the introduction of QCs must be a joint effort where all interested parties are listened to. With suggestion schemes and quality circles the formula may then be, as the Toyota saying has it:

GOOD THINKING GOOD PRODUCTS.

Chapter 21
Education and Training

Although it has been argued that the Japanese have never really come to terms with the outside world, they have generally been successful in their foreign business dealings. Nevertheless, like many countries, now lifestyles have changed, there is a need to revamp their education system. Tomorrow's citizens and managers, on a shrinking planet, will have to be less introspective and they will need to take a more global perspective.

The number of Japanese who go abroad every year is only about 5 per cent of the total population, lower than for any other industrialised nation. This compares with around 45 per cent for England and 15 per cent for the United States. To a degree every country is narcissistic, but the 'Land of the Rising Yen' tends to be more so even though it provides greater financial aid to the Third World than any other. Japan has generally only been interested in another country if there were trade ties. Today on the global scene more is expected of her, and she will need to develop a world role and what can be described as emotional connections with other nations. Indeed, she is already starting to do this with the United States.

But one factor in favour of the Nipponese is that, on leaving school or university, not everyone is clamouring to become a civil servant or to enter a profession. They see industry as being a creative and worthwhile career. In Britain perhaps, someone like Prince Charles, through carefully planned visits, patronage, and by attending social events and making appropriate speeches, could help to reduce the disdain shown among the more gifted for the philistine fields of management and industry. After all, in the United States and France, *business* is, quite rightly, not seen as a dirty word.

A certain Japanese businessman always insists one of the main reasons for his country's success is investment in training. Of course Americans and Europeans also spend enormous amounts, especially in more recent years, but with 'revolving-door employment' there is less inducement to do so. Employers in Japan know, with their lifetime employment, that after a person has attended a course he is unlikely to leave for another job. Also, with promotion based to some degree on seniority, training is more performance oriented rather than promotion oriented as in the West, where, so often after an employee has been on a course at a firm's expense, he or she is expecting a move up the ladder. In Japan, training is often linked to six-monthly performance appraisals. Serious attempts are made to marry individual ambitions with corporate objectives.

When visiting Tokyo with its computer-controlled trains travelling at speeds of 200 kilometres per hour and running every 15 minutes exactly on time, together with other examples of high technology, one cannot help but be impressed except perhaps with the Tokyo cabby who could do with some of the training received by the London taxi driver who has the knowledge and is expert in finding his way. Nevertheless, Japan is efficient and this reflects to a considerable degree their training system and their management of human resources.

When recruiting, emphasis is placed on character and a stable history. Pre-screened candidates are often interviewed by the firm's president. Students from Tokyo University or from one of the other imperial or the handful of top private universities are considered to be the social 'elite' although this does not apply so much now as in the past.

Stress is placed on induction and company loyalty. Welcoming speeches are made by senior staff and newcomers are told how they should accept change, the importance of self-development, and what they must do to follow in their mentor's footsteps. A new recruit is taught how to act according to rank and the situation. Although many girls, for whom the corporate life holds poorer prospects than for men, join a firm hoping to meet eligible bachelors, terrific enthusiasm can build up during initiation ceremonies among both sexes. Sometimes even coloured laser beams have been known to dance, as in a discotheque, and cheering and applause breaks out. Most managements are able to instil a feeling of immensity of purpose as company loyalty takes a firm hold on new recruits.

In their overseas factories, the Japanese also prefer to engage employees when they are young, like 'blank sheets of paper', and interviewees are screened carefully to ensure they have correct attitudes — for example potential team spirit and flexibility. In this way, they can be moulded and made pale imitations of workers in Japan.

Abroad, the Japanese prefer also to set up their own companies from scratch, rather than to take over existing firms with personnel who already have their own established corporate culture which may have evolved over a long period. Employees in such firms are set in their ways. Customs often die hard. When an enterprise has employees with skills which have previously been acquired they do not owe the same allegiance to the new company and it becomes more difficult to introduce Japanese management methods.

In Japan — and sometimes overseas — recruits are taught their company song. This may be sung at the workplace each morning. In the case of one well-known firm it ends with the words,

Grow industry grow, grow, grow;
Harmony and sincerity, Matsushita Electric!

Firms also have their written creeds in which most Japanese employees believe. There are slogans such as:

Let's work together to make our enterprise one of
the best in the world; let's double productivity
through creative thinking and develop new ideas
and original products.

It is generally drummed into recruits, and indeed employees throughout their careers, that the principles of the company are to strive for quality, to be a market leader, to trade ethically, and so forth. Honda's credo proclaims its dedication to:

Supplying products of the highest quality for
worldwide customer service at a reasonable price.

After recruitment, large Japanese corporations provide their own long-term, planned, in-company training, with emphasis on job-rotation, often both nationally and internationally, to produce the well-rounded, widely-experienced manager. Specific tasks and projects are built into training.

The Americans, with their traditions of 'deskilling', mass-production and demarcation, have a history of segmenting tasks. Work has gradually distanced itself from the 'craft' system. The Japanese look at labour with a broader perspective. A trainee may start work in manufacturing — after cleaning company toilets for a couple of weeks or so — then gain experience in purchasing, finance, personnel, sales, public relations, and finish up in the design department. His American counterpart, conversely, may spend all his time on, say, design.

The Japanese aim to train more flexible personnel, with wider horizons, who are less constrained by divisions of labour. Managers are usually given no choice where they are posted and some, if you can gain their confidence, will admit to being in jobs they dislike. The smaller Japanese firm and most Chinese enterprises, as one would expect, have nothing like such attractive training schemes as have the large Japanese *zaibatsu*.

Now too, with greater involvement abroad and government support, Japanese industry has been providing training, sometimes for up to one-year full time, for managers going overseas. Considerable emphasis is placed on improving their English, and trainees also select a study region, usually either North America or Western Europe, and one other zone such as Latin America or the Middle East. These courses have not been well supported. They have been criticised for falling between language and management 'stools'.

A number of Japanese managers attend courses in the United States, not only to master western business strategy, but to establish friendly relations ('networks') with foreigners and to learn about the West. When businessmen are posted overseas they usually precede their wives by about six months, to give husbands an opportunity to overcome any possible cultural shock. Wives are not normally given pre-training.

In addition over 100,000 Japanese managers have passed through 'Hell Schools', which charge high fees.

Their aims are to instil the samurai warrior spirit into trainees and they are bullied in typical, unrelenting, military style. Each day of the two-week course starts at 4.30 am, and, on the 'trip to hell and back', they are subjected to strict discipline, flag-hoisting ceremonies, martial arts, forced night marches of up to forty kilometres (on the lines of 'Outward Bound' schools in the West) and brainwashing. They have to admit their weaknesses.

At the start of the course everyone is given 17 'ribbons of shame' and 'humiliation is used to purify'. 'On the way back to heaven' ribbons are removed. 'Soul-injecting' training is considered important and students learn the school's ten commandments. Naked and without pride they bathe in a communal tub. Everyone is required to make a fool of himself and sing the song, 'You have sweat on your brow', in Japanese, as loudly as possible in a crowded public thoroughfare. Part of it (translated) goes:

You have made the product with the sweat of your
brow,
You have to sell it with the perspiration of your
hands.
What you produce with tears,
You must sell with tears.
Don't feel downhearted salesman ...

and so on, 'singing from the heart'. The performer, blue in the face with effort, is frequently stopped by his superiors and bawled out; 'It's just not good enough, repeat the verse — louder!' The few trainees who resist the indoctrination are told to leave the school while others depart of their own accord. But they know, if they do not complete the course, they quit their company.

A similar programme for American businessmen, modelled on the hell school at the foot of Mount Fuji, has been established in Los Angeles. There students are taught to 'attack objectives as they would the enemy', and, like their counterparts in Japan, emphasis is placed on unfailing obedience, 'we' not 'me', group action, comradeship, punctuality and courtesy. Trainees are challenged physically, mentally and emotionally, and great stress is placed on teamwork and learning through mistakes. The aim is to turn out the 'samurai manager' who is highly disciplined, alert, loyal, powerful and honourable. The course has not been popular in the United States — even though it has been modified to some degree — largely because of cultural differences and misunderstandings. Much of the directly translated English is said to be inappropriate.

Although people complain in Japan that children are not as obedient as they used to be, the toughening process can start at an early age. For example there are a few, so named, 'Sunshine Kindergartens', where five and six year-olds are encouraged to spend the winter in unheated classrooms, stripped to the waist, wearing just gym shorts and plimsolls. They are similarily attired when out in the playground making snowmen. Yes, SAS (Special Air Service) style training can start at an early age!

Though a considerable amount of traditional management education and training is conducted in universities, polytechnics, institutes, management associations, and other public and private bodies in Singapore, Taiwan and Hong Kong, training is not taken to the extremes of the 'hell schools' and induction courses in Japan. But in South Korea, which imitates Japan in many ways, in addition to conventional on and off-the-job management education and training, strenuous efforts are made to fit company employees into the mould of the 'organisation man'. As in Japan, such training can be especially rigorous employing techniques bordering on 'industrial indoctrination'. There are those who believe Korean 'brainwashing' is worse than the Japanese variety.

Because of emphasis on group harmony and face saving in East Asia, 'sensitivity training', in its various forms, is not really appropriate. Situational management training and 'organisation development' must be related, as we learnt long ago, to culture. Not only are Japanese and Chinese cultures quite different to that in the United States, but, to a lesser degree, the latter differs from the culture in Britain, where there are again differences between North and South. Obviously, consideration must be given to culture when planning training.

The 'T Group' ('T' stands for training) was born in the United States in the 1960s. The idea with these 'self-discovery' encounters is for a 'circle' of about eight or ten committed managers deliberately to create conflict among themselves. The participants are allowed to confront any member of the group and to discuss any subject in a 'no holds barred' fashion. While the managers involved in this experience receive the full 'shock' of 'management development' they normally mask their true feelings. The fact that anything may be 'talked through' can provide a valuable, if traumatic, personal learning experience during which awareness of self and sensitivity to others is fostered. Nevertheless, it is often disruptive of personality even though it may bring about a deep, fundamental change. The author remembers feeling absolutely 'drained' after attending a one-and-a-half-day T-Group session in Manchester in 1972. It started slowly, and gradually became more intense as the group continued with its 'creative destruction' until midnight. This brand of intellectual and emotional 'striptease' did not catch on in Europe to the same extent as in the United States.

In 'cross-cultural challenges', when Europeans are working with Japanese and Chinese associates, it is important to remember tradition has it that 'small potatoes' give way to 'big potatoes', and some 'shoe shining' (deference) takes place. Rightly or wrongly, saving the other person's face means you must try all the time to avoid getting into arguments. Even if your subordinate knows you are wrong he is likely to keep quiet or say, 'Yes, I agree, I think so too, but I would have thought that, perhaps, we should have ...' All of a sudden you are given an opening and a chance to change your mind without causing embarrassment. All-important harmony is maintained. Such behaviour, of course, has implications for industrial education.

What is needed in Asia is a more congenial way for people to learn to work together, rather than 'conflict-management training' like 'T groups', so the climate of the organisation is improved. Topics should be discussed and differences aired in a less confrontational fashion so managers' needs and aspirations are better understood, motivation is improved, and there is enhanced efficiency in the group situation. Team building should be fostered.

Even though training may have to be varied to some degree to suit corporate culture, human resources development is important in any organisation. The Japanese believe:

IT IS NOT JUST A CASE OF MAKING PEOPLE WORK HARDER. THE AIM SHOULD BE TO MAKE THEM WORK MORE WISELY.

PART III

危機

CONCLUSIONS

Chapter 22
Recapitulation

Having examined and evaluated management systems of Orient and Occident in detail let us briefly recapitulate. Having already studied our subject, Table 4 is self-explanatory. Japanese methods were originally used to manage an ethnically homogeneous workforce in the home country, where feudal values and the class system had not been replaced by western values. Now, with factories and other assets in the Americas, Europe and elsewhere, and a wide range of foreigners on payrolls, this is no longer the case. As a result different, dynamic management styles and sub-styles have had to evolve in order for them to remain relevant and effective overseas.

We concluded long ago, and it is worth repeating perhaps once more, that Caucasians with our different cultures, beliefs and institutional frameworks cannot follow exactly in Japanese or Chinese footsteps. We have, however, agreed that the management methods of the East are worthy of further research, study, adaption and emulation.

Of course, as we have seen, the Japanese have had to face difficulties abroad. But these have been, or are being, overcome, just as the United States surmounted problems in France when American industry moved into Europe in the 1960s. In the same way, western companies are learning to adjust in Japan.

It was interesting to see, when management consultants A.T. Kearney and Company set about finding the five best factories in Britain in 1989, that two of these firms, Sony manufacturing (UK) and Toshiba Consumer

Table 4: Comparisons of Western and East-Asian management styles - generalisations

Western	East Asian
1. Hierarchical, egalitarian command, segmented concern	Free-form command, roles loosely defined, holistic concern
2. Professional managers, position related to function	Social leaders often with high-sounding titles for low-ranking jobs
3. Particularism, specialised career path possibly with rapid evaluation and promotion, individually oriented	Non-specialised career paths, slow evaluation, regimented promotion, generalism, socially oriented
4. Decentralisation of power	Centralisation of power
5. Mobility	Stability
6. Diversity	Unity
7. Direct approach	Indirect approach
8. Systematic analysis, standardisation, categorisation, classification, conceptualisation, precision	Ambiguity, reaction, adaptation
9. Long-term set planning	Often lack of formal set planning, high flexibility in adjustment
10. Explicit control mechanisms	Implicit control mechanisms
11. Organisations and systems adapt to change	Leaders/managers adapt to change

Products, were Japanese. Details of this survey were recorded in the November 1989 issue of *Management Today*, the journal of the British Institute of Management. To earn its accolade, each factory had to prove it could compete with global best practice in five areas: plant mission, organisation, operations management, quality and technology. The other three firms comprising the five award winners were ICL (International Computers Limited), Rank Xerox and Oxford Automotive.

Similarly Akio Morita, head of Sony Corporation, in 1982 received the Albert Medal of the Royal Society of Arts, 'for outstanding contributions to technological and industrial innovation and management, industrial design, industrial relations and video systems, and the growth of world trade relations'.

The proof of the rice dumpling is, of course, in the eating, and, to quote another example, at Nissan's motor factory at Sunderland, 5,000 workers applied for 250 vacancies. Perhaps, with many unemployed in the north of England, this was not entirely unexpected.

But although some cannot make up their mind whether to love or to hate Japanese methods (Lee Iacocca has made his views clear even if his company, Chrysler, was one of the first joint ventures with the Japanese — in his case Mitsubishi) more and more employees are seeing such companies as desirable employers. For example, one enthusiastic Englishman maintained, 'It's more interesting working in a Japanese firm because you're given greater opportunities and everyone is trying to achieve'. Other more mundane remarks include, 'You are treated fairly', or, 'The Japanese are not necessarily better employers than Westerners but you don't seem to meet so many bad eggs.'

Although there will always be some Occidentals who charge angrily, and others who concede Japanese management is effective, what else has really emerged from our deliberations? With different ethoses in various countries there is certainly no rigid blueprint for instant success. What we imagined to be Mr Lei's 'secrets' of the magic, corporate Orient frequently turn out to be no more than good old-fashioned, common-sense, management. Many good ideas are not revolutionary.

In some cases in Japan they have been copied, in the first place, from the West, and then adapted and improved to suit the East. Some were introduced by the American management consultant, W.E. Edwards Deming, in the 1950s. He is still lauded in Japan, as is Peter Drucker of 'Management by Objective' fame. And here we are advocating copying these methods back again!

Chapter 23
How to Keep One Step Ahead

There have been three major economic empires since the industrial revolution which have exported technology on a world-wide scale: firstly the British, secondly the United States, and now the Japanese. Although international affairs are at present being counterbalanced to some extent by the liberation of Eastern Europe, economic development is swinging towards Asia. We now come full circle back to the title of this book. If the 21st century is not to become the age of Asians what do Westerners need to do to keep one step ahead of the Japanese and the Chinese?

We must initially sit back and take a long-term, detached, 'Japanese look' at ourselves. Not being Oriental there is no need to hide our light under a rattan basket. Firstly, there are many successful American and European companies: there are things we do better than Asians. Westerners need to build on our strengths. We should then, secondly, highlight the strong points of oriental styles and investigate how they can be modified to meet occidental needs. Certainly we should not copy slavishly. Nor should we introduce items just as gimmicks. Without paying too much attention to the exotic in the language and culture of the East, it is important not only to investigate how a Chinese or Japanese firm operates but also, as recorded in this book, why things are done in a given way.

While Japanese travel the world looking for technological developments and new management techniques, which they adopt and match to their own culture, Westerners often delight in giving reasons why their methods would not work in our own case. To paraphrase the centuries-old words of Machiavelli in *Il Principe*:

"There is nothing more difficult to handle ... than introducing a new order. It has for enemies all those who do well out of the old order and has lukewarm supporters among those who will benefit from the new one."

It has been suggested, sometimes with tongue in cheek and usually by the older generation, that the West should return to Victorian values. These, in effect, are in many ways similar to the precepts of Confucianism, and include such characteristics as deference, tolerance, racial unity, a tradition of effort for its own sake, and getting people to pull together.

There are certainly some management functions that the Chinese and Japanese appear to carry out, within cultural limits, better than we do, as we have seen. We should take these and mould them, as far as is practicable, to suit the needs of our own individual company. At the risk of sounding rather vapid Westerners need — as Asians might phrase it — to foster 'a love for our own organisation.'

Even if the Japanese have a talent for being systematic, orderly, and knowing their place, certain characteristics, like openness, individualism, adaptability, flexibility, inventiveness, creativity and physical, social and class mobility all helped to give the West an early technological and economic lead. Advanced engineering skills in Europe, which others copied, evolved and matured over centuries, while natural resources in South America and the Soviet Union remained, to some extent, untapped.

The idea held by North Americans that 'Anything is possible in our great, "young" country', has been a big factor in the development of 'hi-tech', one of the highest of which is space technology, something in which the United States excels. West Germany, too, is past master at creating and exploiting change but the Japanese and the four 'Young Tigers' of East Asia, Taiwan, South Korea, Singapore and Hong Kong, have performed just as well in this regard.

Other reasons for the Japanese success is the immense attention paid to logistics and detail, with their 'decision thinking' and 'bottom-up' style. Contrary to what some commentators say the Japanese do take risks but they are often long-term ones and cannot be construed as hit or miss adventurism. They certainly plan ahead (although flexibility is the keynote), and Konosuke Matsushita, who has been labelled as one of the greatest management thinkers of this century (although, like many other eminent Japanese, little known outside Japan), prepared a 250-year corporate plan for his company, Matsushita Electric. His mission was to be completed in ten phases each of 25 years. But with the average Japanese firm long-term survival, long-term targets, and long-term commitment to both employees and customers are all considered important.

Yet probably the most important contribution to efficiency and secrets of success in East Asian firms is their long-term investment in people at all levels, including building on potential available, the human approach, and the development of relationships and communications.

One of the central purposes of forming groups of operatives into quality control circles is, in fact, involvement. In this way, they are more responsible for the manufacturing and standards of their own products instead of depending upon inspectors to pick out defects. Operatives become part of the management team.

The creation of an employee-oriented management style includes such commonplace items as more training, better working conditions, greater sociability, the development of mutual trust, asking opinions and management and workers moving forward together to achieve common goals. By consciously involving everyone in the affairs of the enterprise, and by providing an appreciation and an understanding of objectives and creating a purpose, the stratification of personnel which retards the operations of many western organisation can be largely avoided.

Chapter 24
The Future

Having come almost to the end of our investigations it would be a good idea to hear a final word from Dick Lei. His father is fond of quoting the Confucian saying, 'Within the four seas all men are brothers.' With Mr Lei senior in mind, it is easy to believe national identities still exist.

Dick is quite different to his father. He believes that the East is becoming more like the West and that as Asian countries modernise, up-to-date technology often demands specific systems of management control. All this helps to bridge the East-West gap. If all communities are to survive and prosper in the next century, instead of the British remaining British, or rather English, they will need to become 'Japish'.

Dick's workplace, with its personal computer and emphasis on information technology, is typical of any modern office whether in Europe, America or Asia. The main difference, in addition to the English variety, is the presence of a typewriter with Chinese characters.

The city-states of Singapore and Hong Kong, with their interface between Asians and Westerners and cross-cultural management styles, including Chinese, Japanese and Western, are ideal laboratories, according to Lei. In the Pacific Century they could become locations where the ideal, packaged, exportable, management style is first developed.

This basic style will need to be adjustable, naturally, to suit local socio-economic conditions around the world.

It will be based on a synthesis of East and West. Dick feels that the Japanese have got to change too. After all by the mid-1990s it has been estimated that the Japanese so called transplant factories in North America will be making over two-million vehicles a year (and Toyota, Nissan and Honda in Britain half a million). In addition, there will be those Japanese cars imported from elsewhere into the United States or Canada. In 1988, the Japanese Ministry of International Trade and Industry (MITI) estimated that Japanese firms employed 250,000 workers in the United States. Another 840,000 such jobs will be created in the 1990s. Several Japanese firms are setting up their own R&D facilities overseas.

Lei believes that Japanese 'Theory Z' has succeeded McGregor's Theory X and Theory Y, and everyone has seen what the Japanese and the offshore Chinese in Singapore, Hong Kong and Taiwan can do. In the next century the Mainland Chinese, with a population of over 1.1 billion, will be on their way. Behold the sleeping giant is awakening! 'Theory C' will come into being along the lines of 'The Doctrine of the Mean', written by Mencius (372 to 289 BC). According to the philosophy of the Chinese philosopher, there is much to be said for following the 'middle path' and blending management methods of East and West. A wide range of permutations are possible. But Lei believes that 'the day when the Chinese lose their Confucianism, then Hong Kong, Singapore and Taiwan will once again become just Third-World countries.'

Another thing is certain, Lei believes. His father and the many small firms around the globe, whether they be European, American, Japanese, or the family run Chinese benevolent autocracies, are going to resist such changes.

When considering convergence of management styles what proportions of eastern and western methods do the ingredients have to be to make for business success? This, of course, depends upon the type of organisation, the business culture, and the environment.

With advancing technology and sometimes greater industrial unrest many western managers have begun to realise it is time for a change. Modern scientific management, which originated from pioneers like Frederick W. Taylor, Henry L. Gantt, and Frank and Lillian Gilbreth, will give way to a new, more international, style.

On the lines of the Japanese system, this must include more involvement by employees, with resulting benefits for the firm, and greater job enrichment. In fact, the emulation and drawing on the strengths, of management methods of the East have already started. Many business groups are undergoing periods of evolution. Changes are bound to continue. But with many sceptics, where workers in British industry may sometimes be likened to the PBI (poor bloody infantry), the process is unfortunately going to be gradual. The fact that, to numerous western businessmen, who should know better, the idea of changing management styles is something to be abhorred, gives indication of the pace at which the upgrading of standards is likely to take place, other than in dynamic organisations.

This outlook contrasts with countless, progressive, young Chinese, like Dick Lei. And, as we soar on towards the 21st century I am convinced we have much to learn from out East-Asian business associates and it is perhaps apposite to contemplate our last Japanese slogan:

COMMITTED TO PEOPLE
COMMITTED TO THE FUTURE.

Glossary

Bushido *	The feudal code of the warrier stressing self-discipline, courage and loyalty
Chaebol ††	Large business house similar to a Japanese zaibatsu
Feng shui †	Sometimes described as geomancy. A pseudo-science which attempts to reconcile the locations of man with environmental 'currents'
Gozensama *	'Mr Morning', a person who comes home late at night after a long day at work or entertaining business associates
Hong †	Large business house
Kaizen *	Seeking to do a job more efficiently
Karaoke *	A kind of entertainment when a group of persons get together for a singsong employing electronic equipment which includes taped music and a screen to display the words and stories relating to the songs.
Kamikaze *	Suicide mission pilots in World War II
Karoshi *	Death from overwork
Kikubari *	Concern, paternalism
Kwai lo †	'Foreign devil', slang for foreigner
Li †	Propriety, norms accepted by society, conforming to a behavioural code which covers commitment, self-restraint, social order, conduct, courtesy, etiquette, tact and ceremony.

* Japanese   † Chinese   †† Korean

117

Lo baak sing †	'Old 100 names', the 'man in the street', the common man
Lo baan †	Boss
Lo shai †	Boss (literally 'old world')
Nam bak hong †	'South-north' firm, originally concerned with the transportation of native products from regions south of the Yangtze River and from North China. Later extended to cover Europe, America and other countries.
Nemawashi *	Consensus building, literally 'digging around the roots before transplanting'
Nokogiri *	A Japanese saw
Onjo-shugi *	An understanding, sympathetic boss
Quanxi †	In Mandarin (*putonghua*), the lingua franca of China, this means a web of 'connections' with a wide variety of people which enables a person to conduct business more efficiently. Similar to 'old boy network' in English.
Ringi *	*Rin* means submitting a proposal and requesting a decision; *Gi* means deliberations and decision
Samurai *	Warrior caste from the 11th to 19th century
Shudanshugi *	Group oriented, the 'We' spirit
Soto *	Outside
Taipan †	'Big boss', chief manager of a large hong. *Di baan* in Cantonese
Tanshin funin *	'Business bachelors', a person who devotes himself to his work
Uchi *	Inside, home

* Japanese　　　† Chinese　　　†† Korean

Wa spirit †	Working together in peace and harmony (pronounced '*woh*' in Cantonese)
Yamato *	The region around Kyoto and Nara said to be the birthplace of the Japanese nation together with its spirit and culture.
Zaibatsu *	A group or combine, comprising a few wealthy families, that controls a number of large industrial establishments or business houses. Zaibatsu were legally disolved after World War II but the idea survives.

* Japanese   † Chinese   †† Korean

Index

About the author

Born in 1920, in Norwich England, Dan Waters has travelled widely and has spent half his life in the Far East. He served in the Middle East as a 'Desert Rat' and in Italy during World War II, and was wounded three times and Mentioned in Dispatches.

The author has worked as a partner and a managing director in the Occident, and he is now a director of a Chinese firm in the Orient. His qualifications, among others, include a Doctorate of Philosophy (economics of technical education), and post-graduate diplomas in management, and industrial education and training. He is a Fellow of the British Institute of Management.

This book draws on his wide experience in business and technical education where he has been a lecturer, a principal, and a planner and an administrator. Since retiring from the Hong Kong Government, in 1981, he has worked as a consultant in education, training and management; he has also written on a wide variety of subjects including management, training, education, industry, general subjects, and teaching technical English.

Dr Waters was made a Companion of the Imperial Service Order by Queen Elizabeth II in 1981. He has served as a Justice of the Peace and speaks Cantonese.

He has also been an all-round sportsman and in his late twenties was an Eastern Countries weightlifting champion in England, he was awarded a Black Belt in Karate at the age of 57, and ran a marathon (42.2 kilometres) when he was 63.